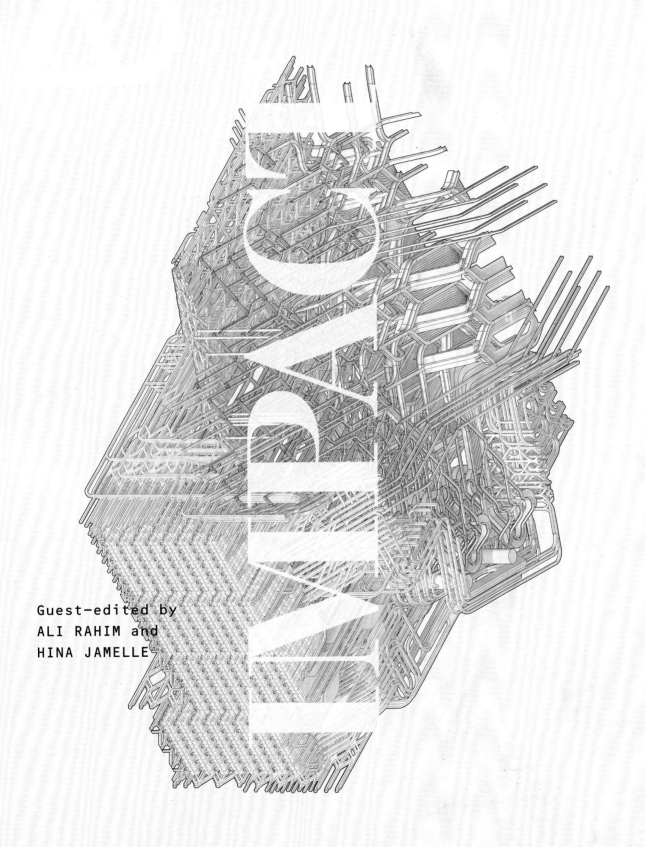

IMPACT

Guest-edited by
ALI RAHIM and
HINA JAMELLE

05 | Vol 90 | 2020

SHoP, Botswana Innovation
Hub, Gaborone, Botswana,
due for completion 2021

Young & Ayata with Michan Architecture,
DL1310 apartments, Mexico City,
2020

ISSN 0003-8504
ISBN 978 1119 651581

Guest-edited by **Ali Rahim and Hina Jamelle**

Editorial Offices
John Wiley & Sons
9600 Garsington Road
Oxford
OX4 2DQ

T +44 (0)1865 776868

Editor
Neil Spiller

Managing Editor
Caroline Ellerby
Caroline Ellerby Publishing

Freelance Contributing Editor
Abigail Grater

Publisher
Paul Sayer

Art Direction + Design
CHK Design:
Christian Küsters
Barbara Nassisi

Production Editor
Elizabeth Gongde

Prepress
Artmedia, London

Printed in Italy by Printer
Trento Srl

Front cover: Caleb White
and Leo Yi-Liang Ko /
Contemporary Architecture
Practice, Style-transfer
techniques using machine
learning, 2019. Image Caleb
White and Leo Yi-Liang
Ko. © Ali Rahim and Hina
Jamelle / Contemporary
Architecture Practice

Inside front cover: Zaha
Hadid Architects, Leeza
SOHO Tower, Beijing, China,
2019. © Hufton + Crow

Page 1: Agata Jakubowska
and Shi Zhang, Future
Airports, MSD-AAD Post
Professional Studio with
Ali Rahim, University of
Pennsylvania Weitzman
School of Design,
Philadelphia, Pennsylvania,
2018. © Ali Rahim

05/2020

ARCHITECTURAL DESIGN

September/October
2020

Profile No.
267

Disclaimer
The Publisher and Editors cannot be held responsible
for errors or any consequences arising from the use
of information contained in this journal; the views and
opinions expressed do not necessarily reflect those of
the Publisher and Editors, neither does the publication
of advertisements constitute any endorsement by
the Publisher and Editors of the products advertised.

Journal Customer Services
For ordering information,
claims and any enquiry
concerning your journal
subscription please go to
www.wileycustomerhelp
.com/ask or contact your
nearest office.

Americas
E: cs-journals@wiley.com
T: +1 877 762 2974

**Europe, Middle East
and Africa**
E: cs-journals@wiley.com
T: +44 (0)1865 778315

Asia Pacific
E: cs-journals@wiley.com
T: +65 6511 8000

Japan (for Japanese-
speaking support)
E: cs-japan@wiley.com
T: +65 6511 8010

Visit our Online Customer
Help available in 7 languages
at www.wileycustomerhelp
.com/ask

Print ISSN: 0003-8504
Online ISSN: 1554-2769

Prices are for six issues
and include postage and
handling charges. Individual-
rate subscriptions must be
paid by personal cheque or
credit card. Individual-rate
subscriptions may not be
resold or used as library
copies.

All prices are subject to
change without notice.

Identification Statement
Periodicals Postage paid
at Rahway, NJ 07065.
Air freight and mailing in
the USA by Mercury Media
Processing, 1850 Elizabeth
Avenue, Suite C, Rahway,
NJ 07065, USA.

USA Postmaster
Please send address changes
to *Architectural Design*,
John Wiley & Sons Inc.,
c/o The Sheridan Press,
PO Box 465, Hanover,
PA 17331, USA

Rights and Permissions
Requests to the Publisher
should be addressed to:
Permissions Department
John Wiley & Sons Ltd
The Atrium
Southern Gate
Chichester
West Sussex PO19 8SQ
UK

F: +44 (0)1243 770 620
E: Permissions@wiley.com

Subscribe to ⱭⒹ
ⱭⒹ is published bimonthly
and is available to purchase
on both a subscription basis
and as individual volumes
at the following prices.

Prices
Individual copies:
£29.99 / US$45.00
Individual issues on
ⱭⒹ App for iPad:
£9.99 / US$13.99
Mailing fees for print
may apply

Annual Subscription Rates
Student: £93 / US$147
print only
Personal: £146 / US$229
print and iPad access
Institutional: £346 / US$646
print or online
Institutional: £433 / US$808
combined print and online
6-issue subscription on
ⱭⒹ App for iPad: £44.99 /
US$64.99

We would like to thank Dean
Fritz Steiner of the University of
Pennsylvania Weitzman School
of Design for his support, and
David Goldblatt, Emily Foster,
Patrick Monte, Leon Yi-Liang
Ko and Caleb White for their
valuable contributions in
making this issue possible.

Ali Rahim and Hina Jamelle's academic research and practice explores the intersection of architecture, technology and contemporary culture. Both teach at the University of Pennsylvania Weitzman School of Design, where Rahim is a full professor and director of the Advanced Architectural Design Program, and Jamelle teaches final-year Graduate Option Studios and directs the Graduate Program's Urban Housing Studios. Rahim has also served as a Studio Zaha Hadid Visiting Professor at the University of Applied Arts Vienna, Louis I Kahn Visiting Professor at Yale University, and as a visiting architecture professor at Harvard University and the Southern California Institute of Architecture (SCI-Arc). Jamelle has held the Visiting Schaffer Practice Professorship at the University of Michigan. They are co-directors of New York- and Shanghai-based architectural firm Contemporary Architecture Practice.

Rahim has published extensively, including the books *Catalytic Formations: Architecture and Digital Design* (Taylor & Francis, 2006), *Turbulence* (WW Norton & Company, 2011), *Asset Architecture* (OROS Editions, 2014), *Asset Architecture No 2* (2015) and *Asset Architecture No 3* (2016). His upcoming books *Future Airports* and *Catalytic Formations 2* will be published this year. He was also the Guest-Editor of 𝝙 *Contemporary Processes in Architecture* (Sept/Oct 2000) and 𝝙 *Contemporary Techniques in Architecture* (Jan/Feb 2002), and with Jamelle of 𝝙 *Elegance* (Jan/Feb 2007). Jamelle's forthcoming book *Under Pressure*, on urban housing, will be published by Routledge in 2021. Both have lectured widely in the US, Europe and Asia.

Founded in 1999, Contemporary Architecture Practice has been known for its futuristic designs using digital techniques and the latest technologies for the design and manufacturing of architecture. The practice's research projects have been funded by organisations including Dupont, Arup, Z-Corporation, ABT Manufacturing and the Wharton Business School. Commissioned projects include the Lutron Tradebooth (New York, 2009), Wall for the Future for the Museum of Modern Art (MoMA) in New York (2008), Reebok flagship store (Shanghai, 2004), Wenjin Hotels VIP Club (2017), NJCTTQ Pharmaceutical Company headquarters (Nanging, 2019), AMEC Technologies headquarters (Shanghai, 2020), Viceroy Hotel (Abu Dhabi, 2009), Samsung Housing Masterplan (Seoul, 2012) and IWI Orthodontics (Tokyo, 2011).

The practice's work has been exhibited at MoMA, the London, Beijing and Shanghai biennales, and the Tel Aviv Museum of Art, among others, and featured in major publications around the world. The firm was awarded the Architecture Record Product of the Month for the Opale light fixture for Lutron's Ivalo Collection, as well as the Outstanding Award for Far Eastern Digital Architecture Design (FEIDAD) for their flagship store. Rahim and Jamelle have also won the Architectural Design Vanguard Award (2004) and in 2005 were featured in Phaidon's *10x10x2* as one of the world's top-100 emerging architects. Their IWI Orthodontics project was featured in Phaidon's *ROOM* (2014) as one of the most creative interior design projects of the century, and they have also been featured in *Fifty Under Fifty: Innovators of the 21st Century* (Images Publishing, 2015). 𝝙

ARCHITECTURAL IMPACT AFTER THE DIGITAL

This issue of _D_ signifies an expansion of the digital discourse that foregrounds the discipline of architecture and its cultural context. When first introduced to architecture in the early 1990s, the digital brought with it a bifurcation of theoretical interests: the material and the immaterial. Design, traditionally guided by the qualitative underpinnings of philosophy, science and the fine arts, was faced with rapid changes in technology conversely guided by quantitative technical measures. Architectural designers borrowed from other disciplines and most neglected their own, while technologists marched towards ever greater efficiency. Efficiency drove architectural discourse towards optimisation and quantitative models often irreconcilable with more robust measures of design intent. Terms like 'blobs', 'nonstandard', 'parametric' and 'organic' all describe the forms that were being generated, which led to a fascination with surface continuity and consolidated in a totalising movement.

However, the success of the digital cannot be measured by its widespread use alone. Commonplace can often become stultifying and it is now time to place impact elsewhere. Over the last 30 years, the digital has been divorced from most of the core issues of the discipline of architecture: how are buildings made in material and detail, what are their spatial configurations, what do they look like, and how do they address and participate in the culture in which they locate themselves? _D Impact_ chronicles projects that bring the extremes of qualitative design and quantitative technologies into close cooperation in service of the discipline. The way to achieve this goal is to implement discrete modelling precision in building design and construction and apply it to disciplinary questions at every level.

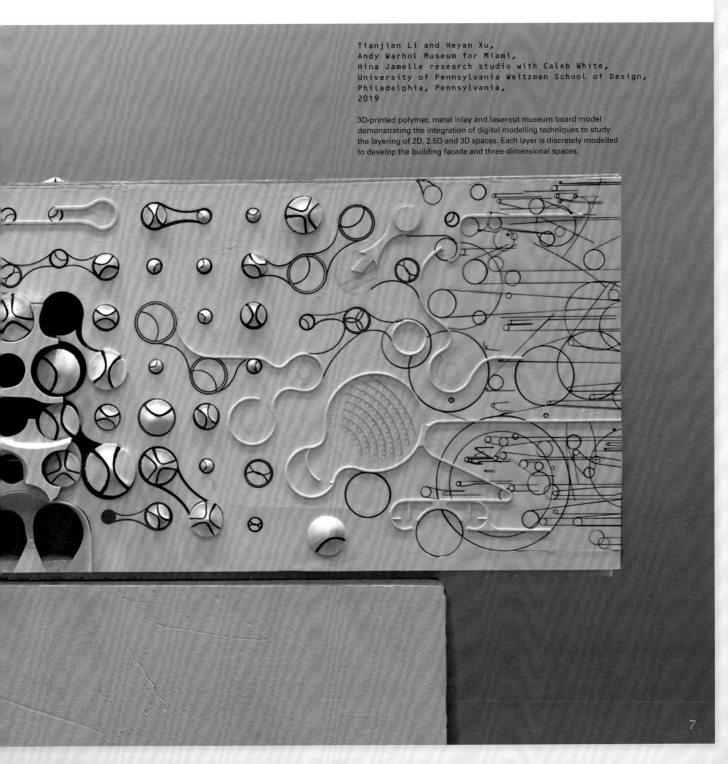

Tianjian Li and Heyan Xu,
Andy Warhol Museum for Miami,
Hina Jamelle research studio with Caleb White,
University of Pennsylvania Weitzman School of Design,
Philadelphia, Pennsylvania,
2019

3D-printed polymer, metal inlay and laser-cut museum board model demonstrating the integration of digital modelling techniques to study the layering of 2D, 2.5D and 3D spaces. Each layer is discretely modelled to develop the building facade and three-dimensional spaces.

Embracing Material Discourse

The issue focuses on material architectural discourse – the things, places, buildings and respective contexts of architecture in the world. There have been two prevalent avenues for disciplinary development of the digital – architecture schools and practice – both of which have at times de-emphasised, overlooked or outright neglected architecture's material reality in favour of advancing technical possibilities and efficiencies. Digital experimentation has had a momentous impact on education. In the predigital modern era, architects were taught to clarify a concept through the design process until it manifested in a building. With the digital turn, this method shifted to an iterative process broadly known as 'design research', which engages making and conceiving simultaneously. In the early 1990s, 3D motion graphics software initially developed to create animation films in Hollywood was introduced in architecture schools. This was the first time that generative computer tools became available to students of architecture, and the shift from the static to the temporal incited a phase of tremendous experimentation.

Architectural design was reconceptualised from the physical site drawn on paper to digital motion vectors modelled in the computer. Serial section projects proliferated and resulted in forms created by interpolating continuous surfaces between sections using Bézier curves, parametric curves introduced in the 1960s for the design of Renault motorcars. Additionally, non-Euclidean (hyperbolic and spherical) geometry led to the exploration of topology – a mathematical concept used in computer script algorithms that replicate natural growth systems using point clouds. Design techniques also transformed in relation to how projects are built. With new modelling, analytic and fabrication techniques available, including discrete modelling, computational fluid dynamics, CNC machining and 3D additive printing, projects within schools of architecture developed into sophisticated proposals for architecture. The possibilities unleashed by these techniques initiated a paradigm shift wherein the building could be viewed not as a complex composition of discrete parts and assemblies, but rather as a monolithic entity unto itself; a new formalism prevailed.

Developments in architectural education were folded into architectural practice along with automation in the construction industry. Large software companies have disseminated standardised techniques for building design and construction based on construction industry products and standards. CATIA, originally developed by Dassault Systèmes for the aerospace industry, was rewritten by Gehry Technologies for Microsoft Windows and enabled contractors to compete in the bidding of complex projects. Building information modelling (BIM) streamlined design and construction processes with automated features and libraries, and powerful BIM tools like Autodesk's Revit became industry standards. Detailing became an automated function of design software rather than a defining feature of architectural design. Broadly speaking, the results have been a sameness in work implementing the same software. Perhaps more significantly, digital architecture has become detached from its materiality and its material consequences in the world. The digital has exhausted its own development and now needs the discipline of architecture as an active partner to develop new material strategies and move beyond quantitative frameworks.

Yingxin Zhang and Lingyun Yang,
Andy Warhol Museum for Miami,
Hina Jamelle research studio
with Caleb White,
University of Pennsylvania
Weitzman School of Design,
Philadelphia, Pennsylvania,
2019

3D-printed polymer and laser-cut museum board model demonstrating the seamless integration of multiple materials to develop a new museum proposal.

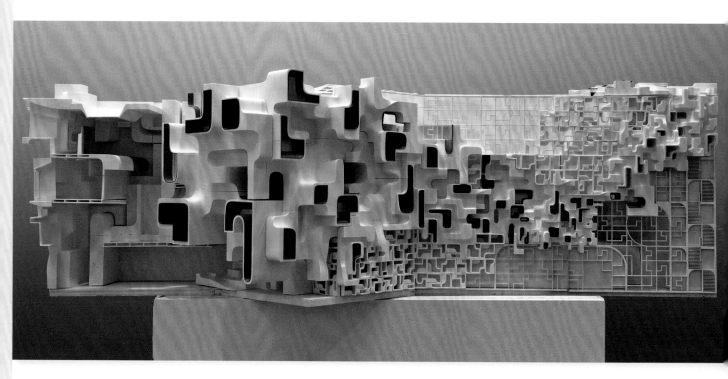

Material Strategies for Digital Design

There are five compelling means by which digital design should materially address core issues of the discipline. First, techniques which are hallmarks of digital processes, if borrowed from other fields, should be narrow in their scope and tested against the discipline of architecture to determine whether or not they have potential for enhancing it. For example, artificial intelligence (AI) and its techniques of machine learning are based on chances of success and accuracy; machine learning trains software to become more efficient at what it does. Applications of AI in urban planning have likewise been efficiency based, aiming to move people around cities in ways that meet the least resistance or enable driverless cars to operate smoothly. Instead of accepting AI at face value for its technological potential, as designers, we should explore qualitative aspects of AI that have greater potential to have material impacts on the discipline.

One such example is the narrower area of AI known as 'style transfer'. Style transfer uses machine-learning algorithms to break an image into two parts: content, the underlying organisation or hierarchical structure of the image, and style, the aesthetic quality of the image. With these two features separated, a designer can apply the aesthetic quality

Xiaoyi Peng and Suwan Park,
Machine-learning image,
Hina Jamelle research studio
with Caleb White,
University of Pennsylvania
Weitzman School of Design,
Philadelphia, Pennsylvania,
2020

Machine-learning style transfer algorithms
with a focus on colour and luminosity used
to produce a new chromatic figuration.

ROBOTIC TECHNOLOGY BASED ON MACHINE LEARNING SHOULD EXPLORE THE REFORMATION OF TOOLS AND TECHNIQUES OF MAKING

Ali Rahim and Hina Jamelle/
Contemporary Architecture Practice,
Machine-learning study for the Wenjin Hotel,
Beijing, China,
2019

Machine learning was used to deepen the practice's exploration of spatial qualities for the project. Continuous discontinuity of colours, textures and materials informed the final design.

of almost any image to another. Though this machine-learning process was initially developed as a tool to maximise image compression efficiency, it has much greater potential to be a qualitative design research tool. This moves machine learning and artificial intelligence from the insulated domain of the computer scientist to the purview of those interested in aesthetics and design. The style transfer technique develops a sensibility for the designer that transcends earlier digital methods, as it harnesses a specific element of AI and focuses it on disciplinary precedents. Such curated architectural applications of AI are investigated by M Casey Rehm in his article in this ⅅ issue (pp 14–21), among others, and show that, rather than just creating infinite variations, robust AI databases can work to deepen architectural knowledge of composition in the building plan, section, elevation or hybridised outcomes and be mined for their architectural usefulness. Likewise, robotic technology based on machine learning should explore the reformation of tools and techniques of making as well as establish new partnerships between digital design and intelligent construction, as exemplified by Philip F Yuan and Keke Li's explorations in robotic masonry (pp 22–9).

Second, advanced digital techniques should be used in such a way that material assembly supersedes the use of digital tools. When transferring a technique from a different field, if the technique is reflected in the geometry of the project, we as designers are relinquishing our responsibility for how that design impacts material discourse. Our responsibility is relinquished to other fields, particularly to computer programmers, who determine the mathematics that generate a surface. If the algorithmic logic of a preprogrammed surface is used to create the material connections and joints of a building, then critical decisions on building construction and core questions of the discipline are relegated to the default software, not the designer. Prescribed operations yield prescribed results. Software defaults should be avoided; they build a precarious discourse for the discipline of architecture.

When the design architect takes control and moves beyond the defaults, their projects have a greater opportunity to benefit the wider culture – to participate in their own materiality – and are not confined as exercises in digitality. How does the architect design the form, space, openings, materials and their assembly, and, overall, how does the building communicate and respond to the culture in which it is situated? These are all disciplinary questions that elude quantitative methods irrespective of advancements in computational modelling. To this end, Ferda Kolatan (pp 40–49) speculates on how architecture might be conceived without origin through entanglement strategies resulting in hybrid entities. Conversely, Hernán Díaz Alonso embraces the constraints of typology through exaggeration in shoe design (pp 50–57), while Kutan Ayata challenges aesthetic assumptions through techniques of material and tectonic estrangement (pp 58–65).

Third, digital design should take on the building at full scale in all its complexities. Until now, projects have been formally and materially bound by restrictive conventional methodologies. The digital project has now moved from the scale of temporary installations and pavilions to that of permanent three-dimensional building-sized fabrications. It should be apparent from 30 years of designing with digital tools that some techniques are not scalable. Much of our time has been spent using digital techniques to design and fabricate pavilions in order to test the veracity of such techniques. While focus on pavilions has advanced design techniques, buildings themselves have been neglected. Buildings have loads, dead and live, and need to be firmly grounded. Buildings require different techniques of making, assembly, detailing, and whole logistical processes that should benefit from the fully fledged experimentation and attention of the digital project. Insular digital projects and their reliance on process to support their vision have created an inflated discourse of architectural imagery that needs to be counterbalanced by a culture of making and material discourse at the building scale. Paolo Pininfarina and Paolo Trevisan's experience in scaling between automotive design and manufacturing and building design are insightful in this respect (see pp 66–71). Further, Patrik Schumacher offers a reconceptualisation of the skyscraper atrium through the realisation of 'the mega-void' in Zaha Hadid Architects' Leeza SOHO Tower project in Beijing (pp 72–81).

Yuanyi Zhou, Wenjia Guo and Qiao Mu,
The Contemporary Detail,
Ali Rahim research studio with
Angela Huang, University of
Pennsylvania Weitzman School of
Design, Philadelphia,
Pennsylvania,
2019

Full-scale research model built to develop the aesthetic of metal folding details and tightly nested metal components. The project developed from the detail to surface to volume, and, ultimately, to a building proposal.

MATERIALS THEMSELVES CAN BE TREATED WITH A WIDE ARRAY OF FINISHES AND TEXTURED IN MULTIPLE DIFFERENT WAYS

Paul McCoy, Molly Zmich and Maria Jose Fuentes,
Design Innovation,
Ali Rahim design seminar,
University of Pennsylvania Weitzman School of Design,
Philadelphia, Pennsylvania,
2019

This multiple-material fabricated prototype questions the role of materiality in the design of a detail or an assembly. Though the model is made of three different materials – CNC-milled foam, 3D-printed polymer and laser-cut MDF – the seams move across these materials to achieve overall coherence.

Fourth, architectural detailing should be reimagined through a contemporary framework. While we attempt to move beyond the aesthetics of the early digital project and re-engage with the intricacy of assembly and materiality, we should be careful not to revert to predigital architectural assumptions. We do not need to adhere to past models of building; the unit of material itself can be modulated, and joinery can be engineered in ways that were previously impossible. Seams can be used to suppress or heighten the tectonic reading of form rather than standardised material sizes and off-the-shelf joinery. Material assemblies can be detailed in ways that differ from area to area, creating highly nuanced multitudinous readings of form. Contemporary fabrication methods allow materials to be assembled and cut in ways that allow for multifaceted orientations. Materials themselves can be treated with a wide array of finishes and textured in multiple different ways. Just as we look to remove the generic digital signature from architecture, we should also remove the generic industrial signatures imposed by manufacturing necessities rather than design intent. Contributions from Thomas Heatherwick (pp 92–99), SHoP's Ascan Mergenthaler (pp 110–117) and the work of Contemporary Architecture Practice (pp 100–109) establish a spectrum of nuanced approaches to architectural craft, materiality, assembly, intricacy and detailing that test and demonstrate new scope for digital design processes.

Fifth, digital architects need to expand their own field of design research to engage with factors including climate change, health, the nonhuman, political economy, racism, sexism, ecology, energy and scarcity of resources – all of which impact material architectural discourse. Antoine Picon's article (pp 118–25) frames the split between technologically motivated digital avant-gardes focused on virtuosity and environmentally concerned factions grounded in sustainability as part of a global shift in the materiality of architecture, which he claims can and must be dissolved through a new ecological view. Broader contextual concerns need to participate in the development of designs in order for projects to be viable. Digital practices would benefit in this respect from the expansive approach required by buildings. Buildings in the public and private sectors are always shaped by many forces, including the monetary capital and institutional structures that fund them. UNStudio's Ben van Berkel outlines ways in which 'disruptive technologies' and user data can be utilised to create new ways of mapping and responding to context (pp 26–33). As a discipline, we can be smarter in the ways we achieve occupant and stakeholder goals as well as our own. Building reuse and the intelligent recycling of buildings are promising examples. Another is the reformulation of asset architecture to provide an investment vehicle for investors while contributing towards city planning goals. Digital designers should further evaluate how their techniques can create new innovative solutions with material impact.

A New Culture of Making

Unless architects turn to a new culture of making, architecture shaped by innovative digital technology will become irrelevant. There are already threads of this argument being made by certain factions of academia.

Atelier Deshaus,
Long Museum West Bund,
Shanghai, China,
2014

Located in the Xuhui District of
Shanghai along the Huangpu
River, the museum site was
once a coal dock. The reuse of
the existing coal hopper and
unloading bridge became central
features of the project and also
informed the concrete materiality
of the museum.

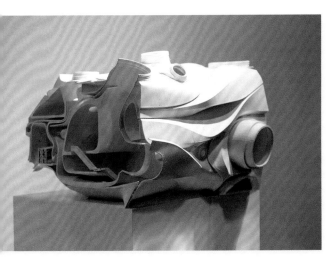

Yuanyi Zhou, Wenjia Guo and Qingyang Li,
Future Airports,
Ali Rahim Advanced Architecture Design studio,
University of Pennsylvania Weitzman School of Design,
Philadelphia, Pennsylvania,
2017

The composite polymer section model shows the aesthetic of a future airport
terminal proposal as well as its sectional strategy. The Modernist airport
typology is questioned to allow the movement of automated logistics systems
through the cargo terminal while also enabling passengers to circulate through
these spaces on their way to their gates.

Critics of digital design at worst seem to assume that we
can naively return to the predigital, and at best appropriate
philosophical concepts rather than dealing with the
discipline of architecture and its material realities. Nostalgic
evaluations should be foregone; the cultural milieu we
live in is digital, and one cannot underplay its impact or
undo what has been done. At the same time, architecture's
complex material interrelations should ground theoretical
positions and be embraced. Digital is where we are, and the
way in which the discipline remains culturally relevant is by
embedding innovations firmly in the culture of making.

This points towards addressing the specific ways in
which buildings are built. The discipline has become
increasingly complex; architects need to grapple with many
materials, structural systems, building systems and their
associated codes. The ability to integrate these into designs,
question their relationships, and shape their flow through
buildings will instantiate a new level of sophistication
in architecture. This can be achieved by using materials,
developing new concepts and means of joinery, and
embracing the discourse's material registration, its impact
in the world. Projects that are more subversive in how
they are created and that eschew their digital signatures
have a greater significance to the discipline's new
materialisations. This issue of ⅅ illustrates these ideas and
their architectural impact. ⅅ

OTHER EXPERTS

DISCIPLINARY AND AESTHETIC IMPACTS OF ARTIFICIAL INTELLIGENCE

enjamin Bratton and M Casey Rehm,
hat Cities See,
outhern California Institute
f Architecture (SCI-Arc),
os Angeles, California,
019

acade texture map study. The elevation is a test on
tilising the image-transforming network developed
or improved augmented-reality tracking to design
n entire facade on a speculative 14-storey urban
negastructure. The volume of the tower was
enerated using a network for translating plans inputs
om the HoaxUrbanism v1.5 into 3D voxel forms.

Constrained artificial intelligence can provide many benefits to the building industry of the 21st century. Los Angeles-based multidisciplinary designer and SCI-Arc tutor **M Casey Rehm** describes how AI, programmed without *a priori* concepts, can develop many previously inconceivable architectural solutions. Such designs do not depend on traditional or received human thought patterns.

Artificial narrow intelligence[1] generates coherent relationships within architecture and its elements while stripping away their disciplinary significance. Embracing the constrained nature of these intelligences rather than attempting to force anthropic metaphors onto their production is critical to extracting new disciplinary value from them. The latter approach leads to false expectations of generative production or creative potential. Instead, the constraints of narrow intelligence allow us to interface both to alternative models of perception and alternative understandings of our disciplinary past. Designing through these constraints produces aesthetics and material orders that defy traditional legibility while exhibiting latent coherence.

Inductive stagnation is the potential trap of any feed-forward intelligence. Inductive stagnation is defined by artist and writer Patricia Reed as 'when "truths" about reality are derived from a set of already known, observable entities, and where that generalized pattern is believed to be true'.[2] It is worth questioning the generative potential of any intelligence that is constructed from large a priori datasets to do more than refine pre-existing design ideas. This refinement has value in the automation of labour, however its momentum ultimately resists a continued innovation in design.

Leveraging Network Structures

Several strategies that resist this stagnation have emerged. One relies on the vastness of the learned features in a neural network to produce Surrealist hybrids between unlike entities with a fidelity of detail resolution that operates outside the aesthetic realms of collage or photomontage. Examples in architecture include the works by Ruy Klein[3] that utilise models created for transferring style features from one image to another[4] to create hybrid architectural images between dissimilar precedents. This approach relies on the extensive features of an image classifier trained on a large dataset like ImageNet to negotiate the disparate image qualities.

Another method is to embrace the constrained understanding of a design space by artificial narrow intelligence to construct alternative disciplinary value. Reed proposes a strategy for socioeconomic innovation based in part on Ray Brassier's philosophical work on nihilism.[5] She argues that to develop truly productive solutions 'we require this productively destructive capacity of reason to demonstrate certain properties of the given as contingent, and therefore subject to transformability, conceptually and materially'.[6] A convolutional neural network is initially an empty structure that evolves its value system from repeated encoding of the given. This gives the network utility for exploring this contingency.

An application of narrow intelligence in art history to treat givens as contingent is the X Degrees of Separation software developed by artist Mario Klingemann and creative developer Simon Doury.[7]

Ishida Rehm Studio,
HoaxUrbanism v1.5,
2018

The grid shows a subset of threshold conditions extracted from Giovanni Battista Piranesi's *Il Campo Marzio dell'Antica Roma* (1762) that was used as a dataset for a plan-generating network. The thresholds have been arranged using t-distributed stochastic neighbour embedding (t-SNE). This algorithm orders images based on the similarity of their embedded feature scores. The scores are then embedded by an image classifier neural network to visualise the model's alternative value system.

The tool creates a new curatorial system for artworks based on the proximity of their embedded scores from an image classifier rather than existing historical frameworks. The meaning of the artworks is contingent on the framework of their evaluation, in this case a machine that can only parse patterns in pixel grids. The resulting connections between works have a visual coherence even if their links sit outside historical art discourse. The value of the app, and others like it, lies in provoking a reconsideration of curatorial practices and a rethinking of aesthetic classifications.

Architectural Applications of Alternative Expert Systems

This application of using networks to construct alternative disciplinary value from architectural givens is explored by Ishida Rehm Studio by mining Giovanni Battista Piranesi's *Il Campo Marzio dell'Antica Roma* (1762) for its architectural elements. Michael Young describes Piranesi's plan as 'the abstract spatial cohesion of the interior created through poché', which 'provides a coherency to the relation between mass and spatial interior'.[8] This observed quality to the poché elements could suggest a reading of the drawing, alternative to Young's object-based approach, as a city produced exclusively through the assembly of architectural interfaces or thresholds. The vast array of poché features in *Il Campo Marzio* stripped of larger formal hierarchies, like axial symmetry, are used by Ishida Rehm Studio in the training of a plan-generating network for speculating on an architecture defined through assembled spatial interfaces, in a continuation of the studio's earlier research project HoaxUrbansim (2016), which utilised similar networks for transforming uninhabited sites into speculative urban plans.

Plan-generation test. The image was produced by a generative network trained on thresholds from *Il Campo Marzio dell'Antica Roma* to create plans from satellite images of unbuilt regions. The plan responds to the features of the input site and attempts to negotiate them with its own understanding of poché/void relationships producing a coherent but illegible order.

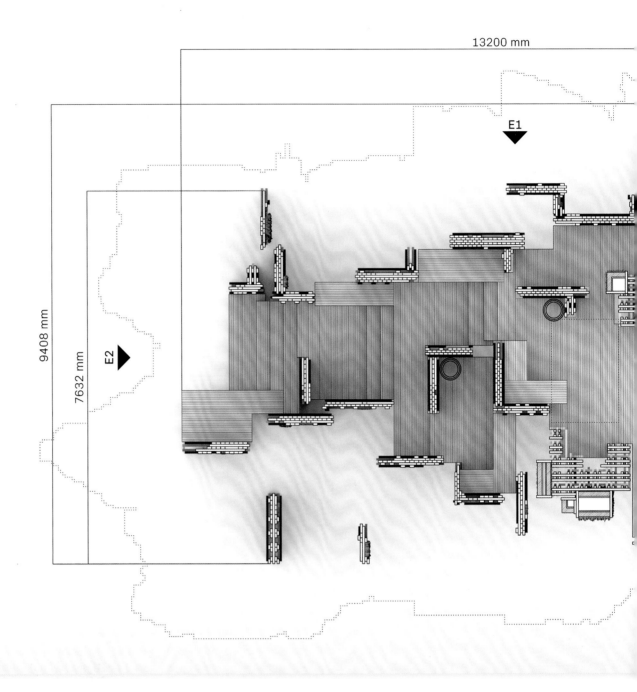

13200 mm

9408 mm

7632 mm

E1

E2

Ishida Rehm Studio with Matthew Lutz, Tallinn Pavilion proposal, 2019

In this shortlisted proposal for the Estonian pavilion for the Tallinn Architecture Biennale, the plan illustrates the ability of a generative neural network to organise wall and poché elements to define a performative relationship between circulatory and static spaces without relying on traditional diagrammatic methods. It is simultaneously viable and un-analysable.

The lamination patterns of the panels are driven by the local needs of aperture, structure and the constraints of the material system

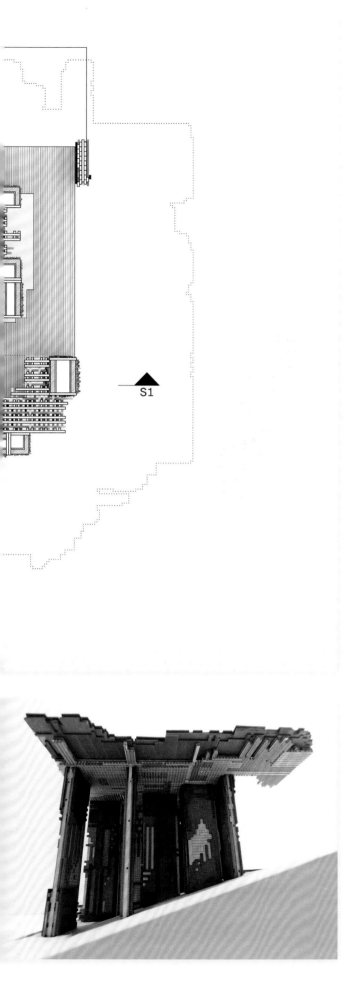

The studio's Tallinn Pavilion proposal for the 2019 Tallinn Architecture Biennale was generated from this network to produce a speculative project on domestic architecture that privileges spatial interface over disciplinary legibility. The pavilion's plan is a region within a transformation of the site by the studio's plan-generating *Campo Marzio* network. When stripped of its ability to understand totalising diagrammatic organisation, the network attempts to create coherent plans purely through its learned understanding of material and void relationships against the constraint of site conditions.

Additional narrow intelligences were used to generate the pavilion's form with robotically assembled cross-laminated timber panels. The lamination patterns of the panels are driven by the local needs of aperture, structure and the constraints of the material system rather than legible compositional strategies. The assembled panels in plan create a layered spatial organisation that is open yet visually opaque. Subspaces within the pavilion are implied through the accumulation of elements arrayed without a legible grid. The use of narrow intelligence allows for an architecture that gains aesthetic coherence through the suggestion of specificity and consistency even if an underlying logic is not visible from a human perspective.

above: Sectional model highlighting the processional effect of the assembled panel elements in defining spaces along the primary staircase of the pavilion. The stairway and the flooring float between the vertical panels like a balloon frame structure, negating the need for fixed levels.

left: Elevational view of the model revealing the differentiated panelling in the proposed robotic CLT lamination pattern, as well as the plan arrangement of the wall panels in the production of layered depth and opacity. The panels vary in thickness and patterning relative to local structural conditions.

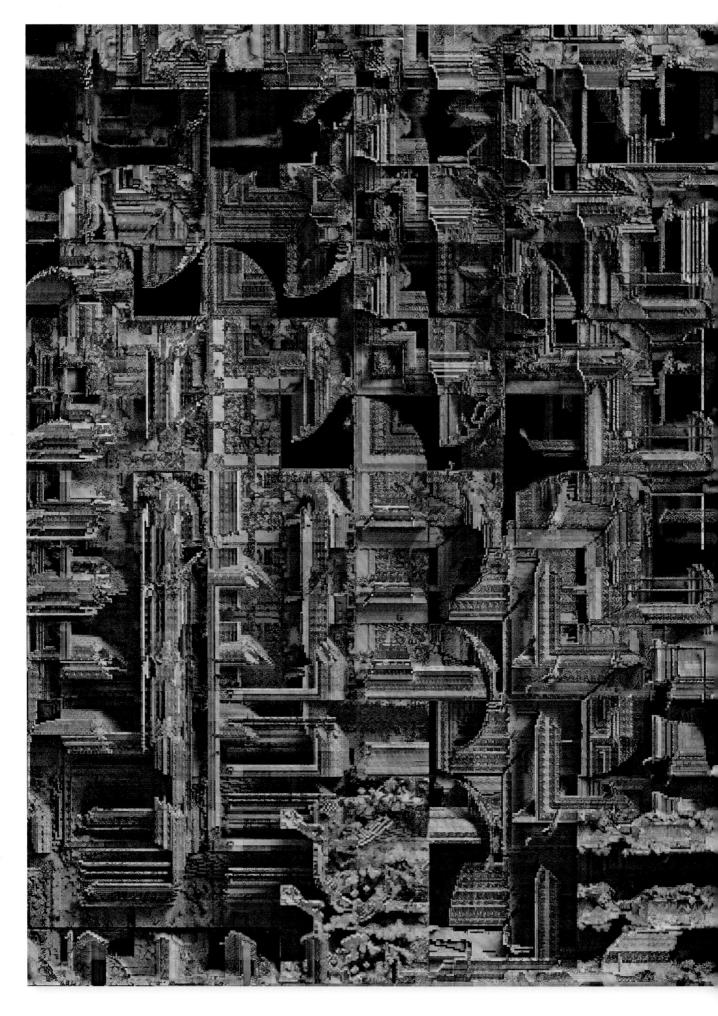

Interface to Nonhuman Perception

The aesthetics of nonhuman utility will become a pervasive aspect of the built environment as continued expansion of tracking and sensing equipment of nonhuman users occurs. The ability of convolutional neural networks to find correlations between images beyond the perceptual capability of humans allows for their use by designers to intuitively engage these alien perspectives. The What Cities See experimental project undertaken in 2019 at the Southern California Institute of Architecture (SCI-Arc) in Los Angeles was funded by the Google Artist and Machine Intelligence group, a programme that brings together artists and engineers to realise projects using machine intelligence. The aim of the project was to utilise adversarial neural networks to redesign urban elements to benefit nonhuman users within a four-block area of downtown LA. The project investigated several types of machine vision, including the LIDAR scanners used by some self-driving cars and image targets for cellphone-based augmented-reality applications. The most effective of the applications was in transforming existing facade elements for improved augmented-reality image tracking. The absurdity of redesigning the city for a rapidly evolving technology like this was accepted by the research team due to the ability to effectively verify and collect datasets for this application.

Benjamin Bratton and M Casey Rehm,
What Cities See,
Southern California Institute
of Architecture (SCI-Arc),
Los Angeles, California,
2019

Opposite: The facade study utilises an adversarial neural network trained to transform the three-dimensional geometry of the 14-storey tower to improve its performance for object tracking with LIDAR. The 3D networks developed for the project are less effective than the 2D networks, resulting in less performative but more alien results.

Below: Augmented-reality tracking panel. The vinyl printed sticker improves the image tracking performance of the facade for apps utilising ARCore, a Google plugin for developing augmented-reality apps on Android platforms. Adversarial neural networks were trained to transform photographs of 0.5-metre poorly performing building surfaces into high-performing trackers.

Photographic samples of 0.5-metre-square portions of ground-level facades in the area were collected and categorised based on the scoring algorithm within Google's ARCore, a plugin for game engine software for developing augmented-reality applications on Android operating systems. An adversarial model was trained to translate a dataset of 1,000 facade samples that scored below 90 towards 1,000 that scored 100. The results of the network at first appeared incoherent. However, in transforming 100 new samples, 98 of them scored the highest rating in tracking software. The vibrant texture and materiality of the panels registers the original facades beneath them, but translates them into jarring compositions. In all cases the aesthetics produced by the network utilised complementary colour schemes and seemingly inconsistent exaggerations of shading. The lack of visually accessible ordering principles in the images make them unlikely to be produced by a human author.

In both the Tallinn Pavilion and What Cities See projects, the exact mechanisms of the design production are opaque to the designer. The narrow intelligences are simultaneously constructed by the designer while also operating as a discrete, inaccessible agency in parallel to them. The pavilion plan defines performative spaces through a seemingly disordered aggregation. The augmented-reality tracking images seem to share qualities of equiluminance and exaggerated figuration, however it would be difficult to develop a specific set of criteria for the transformations created. While these are specific cases, the value of neural networks when attempting to engage alien forms of perception and composition is clear. As design tools, though, they challenge us to accept their apparent effectiveness while their specific behaviours are unauditable beyond a general understanding of the network's structure. To understand the impact of artificial narrow intelligence and specifically convolutional neural networks, we need to embrace their opacity and constraints as opportunities to make our disciplinary givens contingent. ᗯ

Notes

1. Stuart Russell and Peter Norvig, *Artificial Intelligence: A Modern Approach*, Prentice Hall (Englewood Cliffs, NJ), 3rd edition, 2009, pp 34–64.
2. Patricia Reed, 'Making Ready for a Big World', *Making and Breaking*, 1, 2019: https://makingandbreaking.org/article/patricia-reed-making-ready-for-a-big-world/.
3. David Ruy, 'Technological Substrata', The Cooper Union, New York, August 2019: https://youtu.be/TqqDjdWd5EY.
4. Leon A Gatys, Alexander S Ecker and Matthias Bethge, 'A Neural Algorithm of Artistic Style', arXiv.org, 2 September 2015: https://arxiv.org/abs/1508.06576.
5. Ray Brassier, *Nihil Unbound: Enlightenment and Extinction*, Palgrave (New York), 2007.
6. Reed, *op cit*.
7. Mario Klingemann and Simon Doury, 'X Degrees of Separation', March 2018: https://experiments.withgoogle.com/x-degrees-of-separation.
8. Michael Young, 'The Paradigm of Piranesi's Campo Marzio Ichnographia', *SAC Journal: Zero Piranesi*, 5, 2019, pp 57–8.

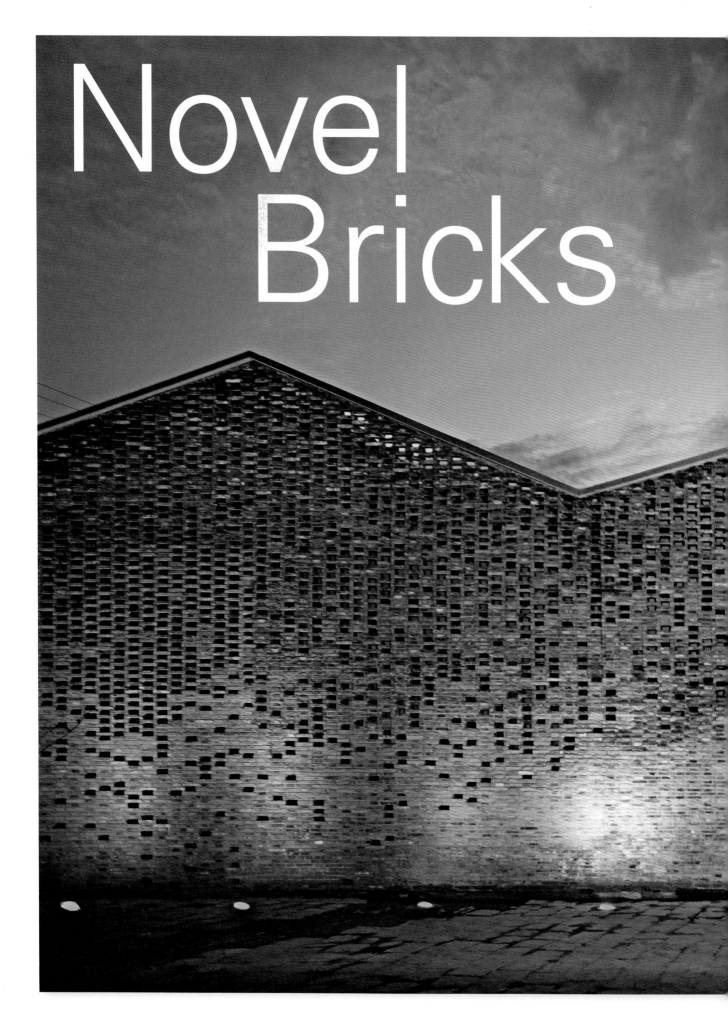

Novel Bricks

A Scenario of Human–Machine Collaboration

Philip F Yuan and Keke Li

Archi-Union Architects
and Fab-Union Technology,
Chi She exhibition space,
Shanghai, China,
2016

As the eponymous home to an art group founded in 1986 by Zhang Peili, Geng Jianyi and others, the Chi She exhibition space is expected to provide an exquisite art venue in the West Bund Culture and Art Pilot Zone. Multiple activities including art exhibitions, collection storage and group discussions are all accommodated within this compact building.

Philip F Yuan, founder of Shanghai-based Archi-Union Architects and Fab-Union Technology, and Tongji University professor and doctoral researcher **Keke Li** develop novel advanced robotic fabrication techniques. Here they combine finite-element analysis, machine vision and robotics to construct a reclaimed brick facade that would be impossible to build manually.

As one of the oldest building materials, brick is still favoured by many in contemporary architectural practice. With the development of structural finite-element analysis, traditional bricks-and-mortar designs can be freed to create new accurate and structural masonry logic.

The construction process for the Chi She exhibition space in Shanghai (2016), developed by Archi-Union Architects and Fab-Union Technology, is an experiment in on-site robotic brick-masonry construction using digital design tools and intelligent robotic equipment. Here, the digitisation of brick-wall construction has inherited traditional building methods while extending their capabilities.

Brick Reborn

The Chi She exhibition space, located along the West Bund of the Huangpu River in the Xuhui district of Shanghai, was originally a service facility for aircraft maintenance for the now long-closed Longhua Airport. The early concept for the project was to enhance the spatial connectivity throughout the site without losing its original qualities or those of the industrial environment. To retain the characteristics of the setting, the existing structure was reinforced. A new brick wall was added to the exterior of the building to reflect the traditions of brick construction in the area and to create a new expression for the building as well.

Recycled brick was selected for the new facade for two primary reasons. Firstly, during the demolition of the Longhua airport facilities, the bricks used in the former buildings were salvaged but unmarked for future use. Reclaiming a portion of these bricks for the new facade was a straightforward way to maintain these historical elements. Moreover, recycled bricks have the ability to harmonise new and old buildings. With the remaining architecture on site largely built of brick, it was the obvious choice of material for the new facade.

The use of the old bricks reflects the designers' sensitivity towards not only the site's history but also the value of creating a new perspective for a traditional material in today's technological culture. Fab-Union Technology adapted robots to employ the reclaimed bricks, creating a new bond between contemporary technology and this historical construction material.

Archi-Union Architects
and Fab-Union Technology,
Chi She exhibition space,
Shanghai, China,
2016

The precision of robotic construction allows for traditional brick to be free in its expression while still meeting modern structural requirements. The worn old brick and the drama of the curved wall complement one another; together they tell a story of humans and bricks, machine and construction, design and culture in the changing shadows of the facade wall.

Shaped by the spatial relationship between the nonlinear geometric definition and the brick parameters, the canopy emerges from the facade.

The old roof structure was replaced with a lighter, more efficient, and warmer tensioned wooden roof. This new roof was partially raised so as to obtain a mezzanine rest space without affecting the spatial relationships throughout the surrounding park.

Multi-objective Generation, Simulation and Optimisation

The design for the facade corresponds with the surrounding atmosphere, blending the humanistic with the landscape, in particular through an undulation that protrudes 1.2 metres (4 feet) out above the entrance like a single giant brushstroke. This discreet undulation acts as a canopy, giving shelter by means of the wall geometry itself. To achieve it, the exterior wall was designed using form-finding software with an added curvature optimisation plug-in.

The specific stepping pattern between bricks was arrived at through the use of genetic algorithms for structural bonding simulations between bricks. Meanwhile, finite-element analysis software was run iteratively to calculate the structural integrity of the brick wall in its entirety. In addition, structural behaviour under wind, earthquake and gravity loads were assessed during the project's development. Through this multi-objective performance optimisation, the non-loadbearing zones, where the bricks could be removed from the facade pattern, were able to be identified. This resulted in a more efficient structural performance and created added visual interest in the facade.

Through the material choice of reused brick, this curved surface integrates digital design with material construction and embodies the combination of digital diagrammatic thinking with machine-learning algorithmic technology. With the material and structural performance optimisation process, there is no distinction between the process of form generation and physical construction.[1]

In-Situ Robotic Brick Masonry

The Chi She exhibition space project demonstrates how architecture can be robotically constructed on site. Through human–machine cooperation, the undulating brick wall was completed with a degree of precision and efficiency unattainable through other means. In this process, the intelligent robotic construction masonry platform, which emerged from the Fab-Union Technology laboratory for the first time, met the challenges and uncertainties of on-site construction. By equipping it with Mecanum wheels, omnidirectional movement became possible. Together with visual recognition capacity and intelligent feedback functions, the platform is capable of accurately placing the reclaimed bricks.

To attain the repeatable precision required of the robotic bricklaying process, additional enhancements to the platform were necessary. During the process of on-site construction, the old bricks, with their considerable size variations, were mechanically fed by a track to a single origin point where the robot could grasp them. Then the robot would scan the brick with an RGB-D camera to determine its geometric boundary. On the basis of this, the visual feedback mechanism would allow the robot to identify the geometric centre of each brick. Combined with the numerically controlled plaster extrusion system, the brick-grasping end-effector would complete the digital fabrication system for synchronous control and accurate construction.

During the construction process, the mortar application and bricklaying were performed automatically by the robot. The structural rebar and masonry pointing processes were, however, completed manually. As technological innovations in construction tools continue, more construction processes will become digital and the possibilities will only increase.

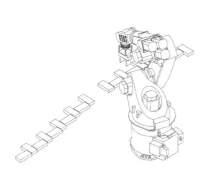

Zero Positioning

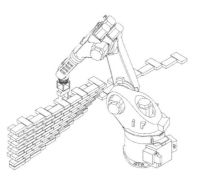

Bricklaying

The complete robotic masonry process consisted of the following steps: positioning the brick at the origin point where it becomes visible to the robot; commencing the construction of one masonry unit; lifting the robot after completing one masonry unit and moving it to the next point for construction of the next masonry unit; and commencing the construction of the new masonry unit.

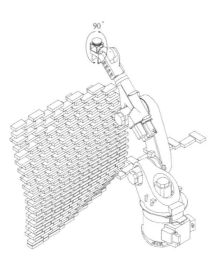

End-Effector Rotation

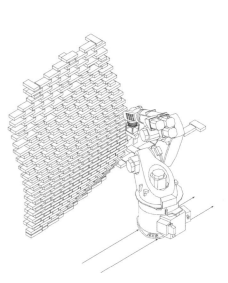

Back to Moving Position

Masonry Future

In this project, digital fabrication and robotic building are actually inextricably linked with a muted sense of nostalgia.[2] Through the combination of reclaimed brick and in-situ robotic brick-masonry technology, the Chi She exhibition space project has accomplished the integration of traditional brick construction with digital tools. The blurring of industry and art, new and old, together with the dialogue between traditional design and digital design form the unique ethos of this completed work. Through parametric design and digital construction, the project addresses the issue of urban micro-renewal in a new and innovative way.[3]

The innovation of robotic construction technology based on machine learning not only explores the reformation of tools, but also establishes a new partnership between digital design and intelligent construction. During the integration process from design to construction, data transmission between machines constitutes a networked feedback relationship throughout every single stage. Machines become not only tools of making, but also tools of thinking. Meanwhile, human beings, as the main subject of design and construction, always maintain an organic cooperative symbiosis with machines.

Though small in architectural scope, the Chi She exhibition space puts the idea of the 'digital Bauhaus'[4] into practice in the ontological sense of architecture. The project takes a solid exploratory step towards digital design and intelligent construction, which turns to be a process marked by innovation in thinking, design, fabrication and tools. New possibilities of collaboration between human and machine challenge traditional design authorship and question authority within the cycle of architectural design and construction.[5] Driven by these new ideas and novel tools, the construction logic of traditional materials like brick may evolve towards multiple dimensions and higher complexities, and ultimately lead to a fundamental paradigm shift.[6] ∆

Notes
1. See Achim Menges, 'Material Computation: Higher Integration in Morphogenetic Design', in Achim Menges (ed), ∆ *Material Computation*, March/April (no 2), 2012, pp 14–21.
2. See Antoine Picon, 'Digital Fabrication, Materiality and Nostalgia', in Mollie Claypool *et al* (eds), *Robotic Building: Architecture in the Age of Automation*, Detail Business Information (Munich), 2019, pp 112–13.
3. See Patrik Schumacher, 'Parametricism: A New Global Style for Architecture and Urban Design', in Neil Leach (ed), ∆ *Digital Cities*, July/August (no 4), 2009, pp 14–23.
4. See Philip F Yuan and Yuchen Hu, 'Exploring Human–Machine Collaboration and Intelligent Construction' (in Chinese), *Architectural Journal: Interpretation of Digitization and Its Technical Recursion Practices*, 5, 2017, pp 24–9.
5. See Mario Carpo, *The Alphabet and the Algorithm*, The MIT Press (Cambridge, MA), 2001, p 117.
6. This article is funded by the Special Funds for State Key R&D Program during the 13th Five-Year Plan Period of China (Grant No 2016YFC0702104), the National Natural Science Foundation of China (Grant No U1913603) and the Sino-German Center Research Program (Grant No GZ1162).

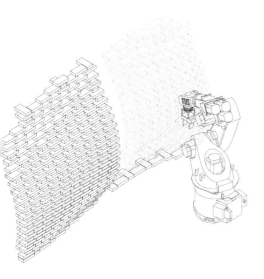

Moving to Next Component

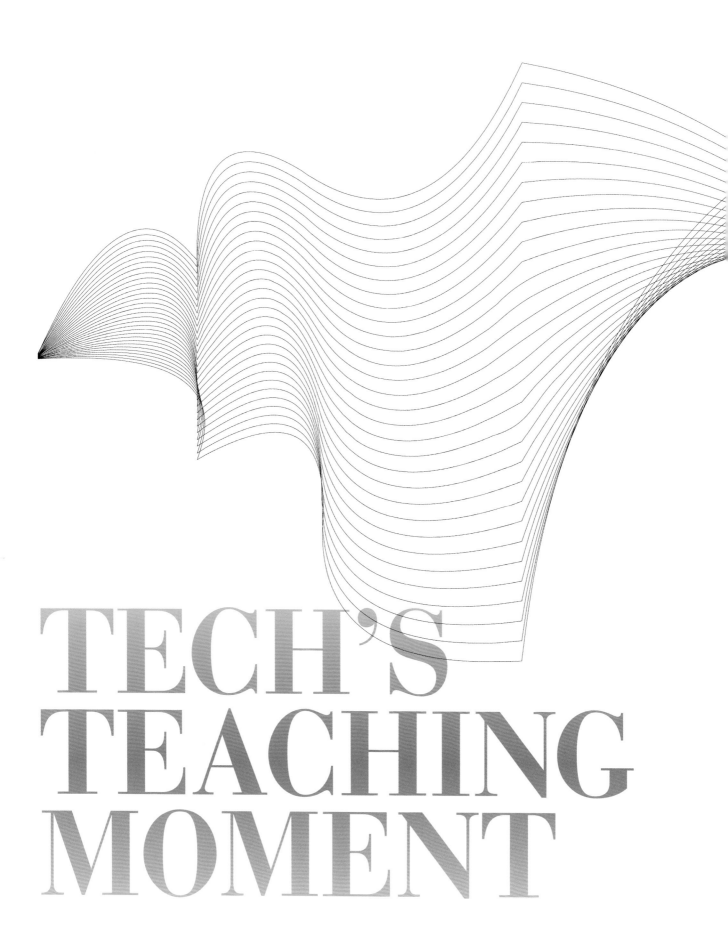

TECH'S TEACHING MOMENT

Philip Nobel

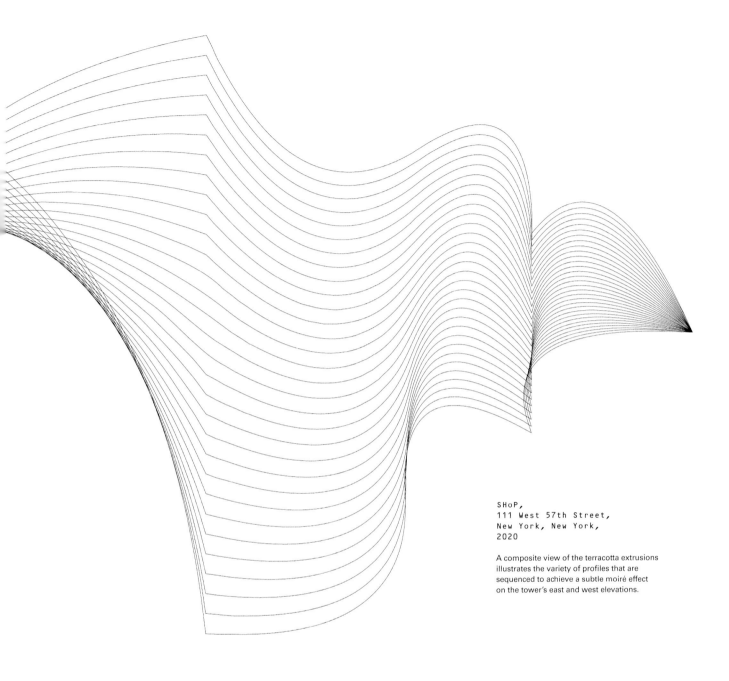

SHoP,
111 West 57th Street,
New York, New York,
2020

A composite view of the terracotta extrusions
illustrates the variety of profiles that are
sequenced to achieve a subtle moiré effect
on the tower's east and west elevations.

THE SHAPE OF CULTURE IN THE POST-BLOB ERA

In the aerospace and automobile industries, while the continuing adoption of digital technologies results in streamlining workflows and procurement practices, faster prototyping and virtual simulations, it has not radically redesigned the form of the car or the shape of an aircraft. In architecture, however, the assimilation of digital technologies has been used to create new forms. **Philip Nobel**, editorial director at SHoP Architects, runs us through the practice's ethos of curiosity and restraint in respect of the digital.

Through more than 20 years of practice, SHoP has taken a critical and often contrary view of the role of technology tools in the design, representation and delivery of architecture. Tech development and experimentation, material and digital, is built into the ethos of the studio – but never for novelty's sake. SHoP is always aware of the allure, even the pitfalls, of new technologies. Innovation at SHoP is in the service of empowering creativity and safeguarding the human element in our designs. The challenge, then, is for the industry to exercise equal parts curiosity and restraint, applying next-generation processes and techniques towards increasing the impact of the built environment on culture.

It has been an imperative for SHoP since the studio's founding in the mid-1990s. At the time, the introduction of desktop digital modelling and early rendering software into schools and select practices was driving primarily formal investigations across the field. This was the heady era of the 'blob' – designs based on irregularly fluid geometries that would have previously disqualified themselves through their inherent imaginal and representational complexity. Now, quite suddenly, these forms could be made readily visible, if not always, or at first very often at all, made real.

This new ability to make it real framed the interest of the young collective. With the creation of buildings rather than imagery as a product of the new tools, SHoP

interrogated each across a very simple set of use-based criteria. It was evident that the initial explosion in the possibilities of representation presented a powerful new means of seduction. Could it also serve more purposeful ends? Ideation? Collaboration? Production?

Non-machine Learning

Looking beyond architecture, we found both inspiration and specific guidance in the technological adoptions of the automobile and aerospace industries. In neither field did digital modelling spur first a carnivalesque of new form; in each, rather, it resulted directly in process innovation. There were newly efficient workflows, stunning applications of visualisation to design iteration, and dramatic improvements to methods of delivery, including in supply-chain structures and their management. Other sectors had incorporated the same family of tools that architecture was first encountering. The result in their industries was to initiate a comprehensive revolution in the degree of both adaptability and control made possible in every part of the creative cycle, from inspiration through design to delivery. Intrigued by what this could make possible in architecture, SHoP then pursued an interlinked series of project-based investigations that, collectively, sought to transfer and incorporate those lessons.

That effort was given a significant boost in recent years when the New York architecture practice was invited by Dassault Systèmes to join a research group that included both Boeing and Tesla. But it began, often well ahead of the availability of optimal technologies to support it, in a series of relatively humble projects that were united by a shared focus on the use of data in the service of production. Among these was *Dunescape*, a temporary installation in 2000 at MoMA PS1 in Queens, New York. To launch the museum's Young Architects Program, SHoP pioneered 1:1-scale templating from digital section drawings, achieving a rapid and inexpensive construction by untrained, volunteer labour – a new mode in public experience with tremendous implications at the literal intersection of architecture and art, design and manufacture, community and culture.

Dunescape established the precedent in many ways for the design of the Barclays Center, New York, in 2012. The client turned to SHoP after a previous project team had failed to rally community approval behind a major urban renewal project, and the 63,000-square-metre (675,000-square-foot) stadium at the centre of a major transportation hub in a beloved Brooklyn neighbourhood appeared to be another point of contention. Faced with that late arrival to the process – and an immovable deadline tied to the tip-off of the NBA basketball season, as well as a series of already sold-out Jay-Z shows – SHoP pioneered an integrated direct-to-fabrication manufacture and delivery process that allowed the now-iconic building to be completed with no sacrifice to its complex architectural expression, and a new cultural centre for the neighbourhood.

Also evident to different degrees in the later, larger arena are several other early SHoP 'DNA' projects: the Porter House in Manhattan, a residential renovation completed in 2003 and the first instance of direct-to-fabrication in a commercial facade that prefigured the transformation of the Meatpacking District; and the Camera Obscura, the centrepiece of the 2005 work the studio did to assist the cultural, civic and economic transformation of Greenport, a seaport town on the North Fork of Long Island. Through a pre-emptive, brute-force use of virtual design and construction (VDC) technology *avant la lettre*, SHoP modelled each direct-fabricated part 'by hand' to eliminate all cutting and measuring on site.

The Tools To Pick Up (And Put Down)

Today, SHoP's in-house research and implementation continues across a broad front, with projects underway to apply virtual and augmented reality to both architectural design and its efficient delivery, a years-long and accelerating initiative to reimagine the architectural supply chain, and the active adaptation of VDC to urban masterplanning together perhaps serving to frame a general scope.

When we integrate them into our processes, we see them always as tools, subservient to intent. Even as the decades have passed, as emergent softwares are fruitfully repurposed and integrated in-house, as the new machines we unbox in our studios double and redouble again in their power and possibility, we maintain that critical distance. Just as we never wanted our pencils to be dragging our hands across the page, we do not allow our digital technologies to dictate or foreclose what is possible.

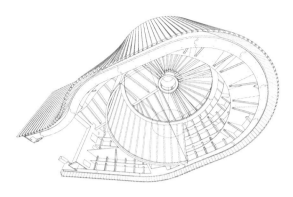

SHoP,
Camera Obscura,
Mitchell Park, Greenport,
Long Island, New York,
2005

The Camera Obscura's all-digital delivery made possible the rapid, exact, affordable construction of an irregular geometry comprising 1,487 unique pieces.

SHoP,
The Porter House,
New York, New York,
2003

below: In designing the zinc rain-screen facade of the Porter House, industrial nesting software maximised panel variation while minimising material waste.

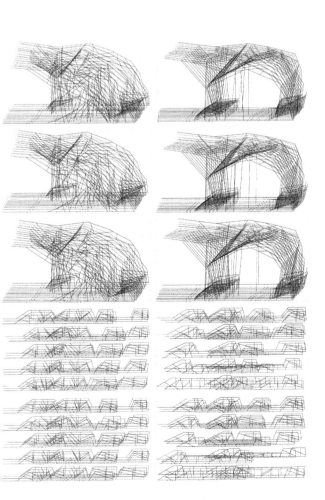

SHoP,
Dunescape,
Long Island City,
Queens, New York,
2000

left: Composite of the drawings used in the field as templates in the assembly of *Dunescape*, an installation at MoMA PS1 that featured rapid, low-cost construction by untrained volunteers.

Purposeful Applications

Perhaps no recent project represents the SHoP application of technology to accelerate cultural impact better than the Botswana Innovation Hub (BIH), with expected completion in 2021. The site, in the capital Gaborone, is a somewhat marginal one, on the scrubby outskirts where the sprawling city meets the long horizons of the Kalahari Desert. Its purpose, however, is central to the future social and economic wellbeing of that country. The genesis of the project was in a government initiative to plan ways forward for Botswana beyond a narrow reliance on the diamond trade.

One of several hubs mandated by the government to encourage education and entrepreneurship in various alternative industrial sectors, BIH was conceived as both an incubator and a laboratory, with tenants to include leading global technology firms, enterprises in the biological sciences, workspace and support facilities for startups in related fields, and the offices of the public agencies that will foster them over the long term. The zone surrounding the hub, which SHoP also planned, is slated to host freestanding facilities for the businesses that grow up within and eventually graduate from the central complex itself.

SHoP,
Botswana Innovation Hub,
Gaborone, Botswana,
due for completion 2021

Sited where Gaborone meets the Kalahari Desert, Botswana Innovation Hub (BIH) is a foundational component of a national programme to encourage technological education, innovation and entrepreneurship.

With this brief in hand, after SHoP won the commission through an open competition, it was evident that a certain amount of forward-facing technologies were inherent to our clients' mission. Innovation authentically developed and applied informed the mood and meaning of the building. The architecture evolved through site and climate considerations into a low-slung complex of three long wings, each under a xeriscaped, energy blanket roof, the whole strategically connected across shaded, open courts in a pattern of circulation between shared amenities intended to promote serendipitous encounters between all entities. That desire to invite the convergence of ideas shaped the building as it stood in schematic design. It also pointed the way to the most fruitful approach to applying our technology.

Beginning in 2014, SHoP instituted a programme of rotating the New York City-based project team through staggered six-week residencies in Gaborone. Internally and externally, the goal was education. To give our associates an opportunity to learn – about Botswana, of course, and the challenges of international construction in general, but also directly, at a more personal level, from our local partners and contractors on the project.

The form of BIH's facades is determined by the need to reduce sometimes heavy heat loads via self-shading.

A series of open courts create beneficial microclimates that are thickly planted to encourage outdoor gathering.

SHoP,
Botswana Innovation Hub,
Gaborone, Botswana,
due for completion 2021

View of the unfinished main lobby
interior showing one of the murals
created using a traditional applied-
earth technique.

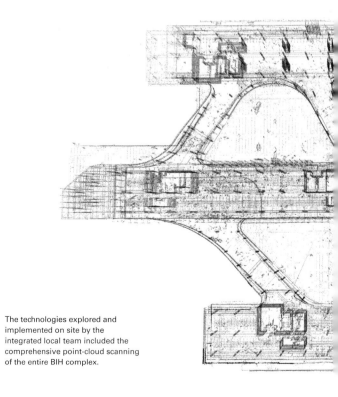

The technologies explored and
implemented on site by the
integrated local team included the
comprehensive point-cloud scanning
of the entire BIH complex.

We were cognisant of the challenges in building so intimately for a place and a culture with which we had so little familiarity. We wanted to reduce that gap, as well as the possibilities of instantiating a latent colonialism, or merely a gross architectural error of the type that cultural arrogance can so often produce.

One result of this immersion was our team making the acquaintance of Peter Mabeo, Gaborone-born furniture designer and founder of the eponymous international brand. He soon became deeply involved with the project, interpreting in wood several critical parametrically designed systems for the interior and producing them from our digital models in his factory not far from the site. He became an essential connection as well to a network of other local artisans who took on the design and production of finishes ranging from tile work to traditional earthen-fresco murals.

In the spirit of beginning the work of technological and cultural cross-pollination that is at the heart of the Hub's own mission, SHoP also saw this project as an opportunity for in-process learning, to introduce some of the more rarefied methods that had proven useful closer to home, and to test them for transferability and solipsism in this new context. Over the years, the long table in the construction trailer became an ongoing point of exchange in the direct application of contemporary architectural technologies between the local team and local collaborators. A web-based system SHoP developed in-house in Manhattan for remote interaction with a digital twin was first field tested in Gaborone, for instance. The combined team discovered, among other uses, the utility of such advanced modelling in clash detection, with project information generated and confirmed directly on site via smartphone.

As the Botswana Innovation Hub approaches completion and the New York-based team has been recalled and moved on to other work, SHoP has been able to hand over to partners in Gaborone the completion of the entire digitally delivered self-shading facade system – a cutting-edge VDC-driven direct-to-fabrication program that dwarfs the effort at Barclays Center in both its element count and its inherent complexity. This manner of delivery allowed SHoP to generate a fully automated instruction set in the form of 'fab tickets' and directly output as mass-customised aluminium components in southern Africa. On site, they are achieving an installation with millimetre tolerances. It is an added benefit that the fabrication house we worked with will be able to apply this highly adaptable and efficient method to future projects to meet urgent construction needs across the region.

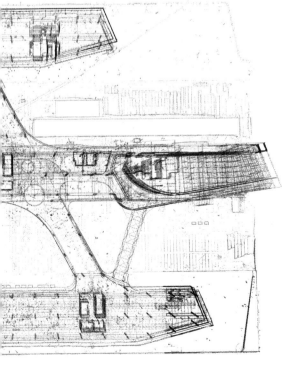

SHoP,
111 West 57th Street,
New York, New York,
2020

Traditionally built, with
technological support primarily in
the development of the terracotta
facade system, 111 West 57th
Street demonstrates the strategic
use of tools.

Tall Order

Another relevant current project, its definitive impact vertical to the Botswana project's horizontal reach, is our residential tower at 111 West 57th Street in Manhattan, expected to be complete by the end of 2020. With a height of 435 metres (1,427 feet) and a width of only 18 ('59), its aspect ratio of 1:24 makes it the most slender tall building in the world. In many ways, however, it is also very traditional; 111 West 57th serves to demonstrate the SHoP commitment to the strategic, often sparing, use of technology tools, calibrated to support each project's design and cultural objectives.

For decades the international cadres of skyscraper engineers have had the methods and processes in hand to build up and up, even to go to and past the romantic limit of one mile high. They were waiting only for the convergence of economics and will that would make such an effort possible. West 57th Street is one such place. There, the ambient intensities of the Manhattan residential market aligned with an influx of international real-estate capital, good bedrock, and the proximity to Central Park to create a dotted line of new view-capturing luxury supertalls. Zoning practices peculiar to New York contribute as well: each tower gathers up and transfers the available 'unoccupied' sky above the lower adjacent buildings (the air rights), and so, paradoxically, ensures for some time a high degree of picturesque variation on the skyline.

To contribute to this cityscape, SHoP was asked to prepare a design for the very narrow site immediately adjacent to, and partially overlapping with, one of the more treasured buildings on the street: Steinway Hall, built in 1925 by Warren & Wetmore. With its significant historical status, a confirmed landmark inside and out, any new construction had to be focused on generating a meaningful compatibility.

The SHoP team welcomed that necessity, too, as New Yorkers. The great architectural symbol of Manhattan is not any single stand-out building, but all of them, in their amassed and silhouetted collectivity. Any new tower that breaks into the hallowed zone of the public skyline bears an enormous responsibility to do so with a sense of deference to the entirety of that elevated context, so synonymous with the cultural identity of the city. SHoP added to this understanding a hometown desire to honour the heritage of the city as a birthplace of the skyscraper form. We wished to crack the code and create a place-heralding design, one that would embody a site-specific expression that would feel out of place if it were to be transferred, as is so common today, to a very different context across the globe.

With those goals in mind, SHoP focused on material explorations, eventually consolidating our interest in the possibilities of terracotta – one of the oldest construction materials still in active use, arguably underused through recent decades. The enduring favourite from the classic age of the New York skyscraper, we discovered, through direct experimentation and consultation with noted fabricators, was also eminently adaptable to the forms made possible by contemporary digital modelling software.

THE GREAT ARCHITECTURAL SYMBOL OF MANHATTAN IS NOT ANY SINGLE STAND-OUT BUILDING, BUT ALL OF THEM, IN THEIR AMASSED AND SILHOUETTED COLLECTIVITY

High Culture

The tower itself was resolved architecturally using Revit, a somewhat outdated platform but one optimised for iterative vertical extrusion. The structural requirements of the tower, however, presented another opportunity. The need to retain the spatial clarity of the interior, as well as counter significant wind-loading, demanded the use of full-length shear walls along the deepest dimensions of the tower east and west. These were also the elevations that would become most visible, following the peculiar dynamics of Manhattan sight lines, to all but the most distant observers. Those same walls, SHoP discovered, could be clad with a series of pilasters, each rising unbroken to meet one of the many set-backs that defer to a zoning-mandated sky plane – giving the tower a distinctive feathered silhouette and uniting its vertical surfaces with its overall form.

Here the team continued, using Grasshopper to script various profiles and offsets for the terracotta pilasters, eventually refining these investigations into a design that used several dozen profiles in a repeating series, staggered across the facade to create a sweeping moiré pattern at the city scale. Over the course of a given series, the profiles range from open and gently rippled to progressively deeper and more pronounced in their modelling. At their most involute they offer a little treat for the keen architectural observer. In elevation they are vaguely classical, if somewhat asymmetrically baroque.

But in cross-section they take on a look similar to the blob geometries from the 1990s, those characteristic forms that marked a certain subset of architectural production at the moment when the field first adopted – but had not yet learned to control – its powerful digital toolset and the enduring impact it would have on the thrilling invention and reinvention of the urban landscape and the culture it generates and serves. ◌

Ferda Kolatan

Genuine Hybrids

Towards an Architecture with No Origin

SU11 Architecture + Design,
Coral Column,
2016

opposite: An important and typical characteristic of the Genuine Hybrid is its play on dichotomic relationships such as real/copy or mundane/precious. The extruded and printed parts of the column mirror each other and reverse effects that are commonly associated with a particular material or fabrication technique.

Co-founder of SU11 Architecture + Design, and Associate Professor of Practice at the University of Pennsylvania, **Ferda Kolatan** postulates the idea that 'authenticity' with its assumed single point of origin is impossible in our contemporary culture, where all is a series of hybrid mixtures and variations, and the raw material of further architectural appropriation and adaption.

SU11 Architecture + Design, Coral Column, 2016

Coral Column was developed for the exhibition 'Close-Up' at the SCI-Arc Gallery, Los Angeles, California in 2016. The exhibition brief called for projects examining the impact of digital technologies on the architectural detail and the traditions of tectonic expressions associated with it.

Can there be an authentic architecture with no origin? At first this question may appear absurd as authenticity seems unthinkable without originality. The Merriam-Webster dictionary defines authenticity as 'conforming to an original so as to reproduce essential features' and as 'worthy of acceptance or belief as conforming to or based on fact'. According to this commonly accepted definition, the authentic cannot just come into existence without a prior original to which it conforms. Furthermore, Merriam-Webster's definition implies that 'original' and 'fact' are largely interchangeable terms with 'essential features', which establish the blueprint for the authentic. It follows, then, that for something to be authentic it needs to accurately reproduce an original or a fact, and failure to do so will result in a 'copy' or a 'fake'.

This definition, however, of a slavish authentic with an unquestionable factual origin seems rather at odds with our current culture and its proclivity for digital image reproduction and proliferation. After all, to define any true origin becomes increasingly pointless in a milieu where ideas of the singular, pure or essential are overwhelmed by an onslaught of variations, mixtures and duplicates across ever-multiplying media platforms. But this does not necessarily mean the obsolescence of authenticity itself, be it as a concept or value system. As it turns out, our fervour to valorise, dismiss and generally make qualitative judgements about digital images has not diminished at all by vanishing origins. The world has not flattened into a plane made of indistinguishable replicas with no inherent value, but instead a whole new class of objects with hybrid qualities (digital images) has emerged.

Perhaps, then, we need to redefine the meaning of authenticity in our current age and ask how it functions as a value system liberated from concepts of originality. 'Genuine Hybrids', a deliberate oxymoron, seek to overcome perceived contradictions between qualities we commonly describe as honest, unique or real and those that are ambiguous or fictitious. It also promotes a design thinking that actively integrates the cultural effects of digital proliferation into the material practice of architecture. For if digital image culture, which increasingly governs our daily experience, is indeed transforming such fundamental concepts as authenticity and originality, then our views of what constitutes value in the physical world and how architecture can manifest it are likely to be impacted as well.

An Ecology of Cross-Categorical Entanglement

The processes of compressing objects, architectural or otherwise, into digital images, and their subsequent dissemination and reimaging into myriads of 'copies' or alternative versions, likely marks an irreversible departure from past concepts of origin. When in the 1930s Walter Benjamin bemoaned the loss of an object's aura, its uprooting from the 'here and now'[1] through technological reproduction, the successive steps from object to machine to image were still comprehensible in their causality. The gravitational weight of the original object was still very much intact, it could be pointed to and contrasted in a meaningful way against its own copy. In other words, the original could resist because it was anchored within a specific context, while the copy – in Benjamin's argument – became exploitable as 'propaganda' because it was not.

Today, however, we are fully immersed in and consumed by digitised images of objects (and of other images), which are not simply uprooted from their origin or context, but actively engaged in a deliriously rapid reproduction of their own. The sheer number of endless versions and alterations, caused by digital transfer or deliberate human interaction, render impossible any attempt to tie these images to a singular context or determine their originality. But this fact, ironically, sets the stage for the copy to be reverted into a new original of sorts. By lacking a clear reference to a distinct point of origin, the image-object gains enough autonomy to engage in unexpected and novel combinations and collaborations. And at this juncture, where liberated images re-originate into new coherences through acts of mixing and hybridisation, our perception of copies as diminished, second-hand cultural objects may need to be reversed.

To seize on this reversal and to mine its potential for our field we must ask how image-based hybrids can re-enter the material world productively as architecture. Furthermore, we need to illustrate that appropriating existing objects can indeed produce novelty rather than exhaust itself in arbitrary reshuffling, or worse, become a form of underhanded plagiarism. These issues are ultimately about design rather than technology or representation. They prompt us to envisage a built environment where uprooted artefacts form new alliances, which become significant by transposing digital phenomena into the

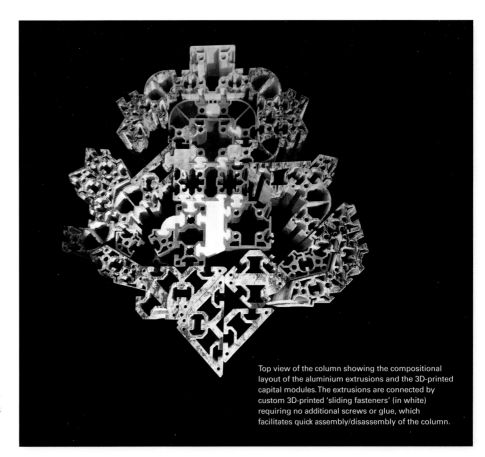

Top view of the column showing the compositional layout of the aluminium extrusions and the 3D-printed capital modules. The extrusions are connected by custom 3D-printed 'sliding fasteners' (in white) requiring no additional screws or glue, which facilitates quick assembly/disassembly of the column.

analogue world and vice versa. To achieve this, however, it is necessary to move beyond the notion of the digital as primarily a tool and instead understand it in terms of an ecology, one in which different technological, cultural and material capacities would continually exchange, intertwine and entangle with each other and with us.

In this new ecology, categorical divisions hailing from the Enlightenment era and meant to classify, order and purify the world into 'rational' segments no longer apply. Oppositional realms neatly constructed from pairings such as original/copy, object/image or real/fiction simply no longer function as registers for the principal conditions of contemporary life. Rather, they have become vestiges of a time when a clear distance between these oppositional terms was assumed to exist. The current dissolution of this assumption and the collapse of these dichotomies has created the kind of territory in which unprecedented cross-categorical interactions and transformations can form. Herein may just lie the most radical change ushered in by digital media to date.

Two case studies illustrate how these ideas can directly inform design. Each privileges an ecology of cross-categorical entanglement as the conceptual departure point for an authentic architecture with no origin. And both examine, in very different formats and scales, how this approach can foster a multifaceted architecture that engages the observer and their cultural environment through specific references to place, time and fabrication techniques that are remixed and take on new meanings as Genuine Hybrids.

Allusive Object

SU11 Architecture + Design's project Coral Column (2016) is a sculpture in the form of a column. Or rather, it is an object alluding to the properties and features commonly associated with columns. For instance, it is visually separated into three parts, much like the base, shaft and capital of classical column orders. The shaft is constructed by a planar array of several stock aluminium extrusions into a single solid core. Between each extrusion a narrow vertical gap is formed, vaguely reminiscent of linear fluting in columns of bygone periods. Further below at the base, the extrusions are diagonally sliced off, revealing an ornamental pattern caused by the profiles' usually hidden, finely structured webbing. Atop the aluminium core, like a crown, 3D-printed elements assemble a richly decorated capital that appears both marble-like and coralline.

left: The Coral Column's base reveals more intricate patterning exposed by diagonal slicing techniques. The differentiation of the column into base, shaft and capital is an attempt to mix contemporary aesthetics with historical references to classical column orders.

below: The 'ornamental' pattern is exposed by an oblique cut of the aluminium extrusion's structural webbing. The image shows how the patterns transition into the capital.

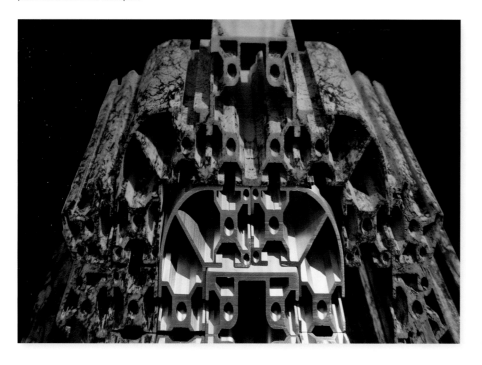

The interplay between revealing and hiding, the multiple references across time and culture, and the tension created by contrasting fabrication techniques are the defining qualities of Coral Column. A set of three dichotomies – digital/analogue, precious/mundane and figural/abstract – are challenged to engage in unexpected and non-binary combinations. For example, by obliquely slicing the aluminium extrusions patterns are revealed, which in their complexity evoke a digital signature. In turn, the colour and patterning of the actual digital capital displays the visceral quality and heft of a rock, while also replicating the extrusion structure. As a result, the functional webbing inside the profiles assumes now an ornamental role and enmeshes mundane features with those we habitually consider precious. In yet another reversal, glue and powder with a monetary value far below that of standardised aluminium form the richly articulated and 'precious' crown of the capital.

Another demonstration for an unexpected collaborative cohesion across categorical lines is manifested in the column's figurative and abstract properties. The aluminium extrusion is a classic example of the modern ethos of standardisation. The profiles are considered 'abstract' because a machine produced them, creating a formal language distinct from that of a craftsperson. But the selection of the individual profile types, their composition into the planar array and the oblique cuts are all 'figurative' in that they were driven to express form independent of utility.

The ensuing tension between an abstract aesthetic derived from a strict adherence to fabrication techniques and an aesthetic of local and deliberate effects expands further on the tension between the digital and the analogue qualities of the column. Over millennia, and probably more than any other building component, the column has functioned as a typological marker for stylistic and ideological shifts in culture. A given era's values and ideas were reflected in proportion, detail and ornament. In mixing stylistic, historical and material features, Coral Column signals a cultural shift as well, one that moves away from hardened categories of division and towards new forms of hybridisation. As illustrated by the shortened shaft and the mirrored base, Coral Column is a sculpture, a standalone artefact. But the qualities it exhibits, and the questions it touches on squarely belong to the realm of architecture.

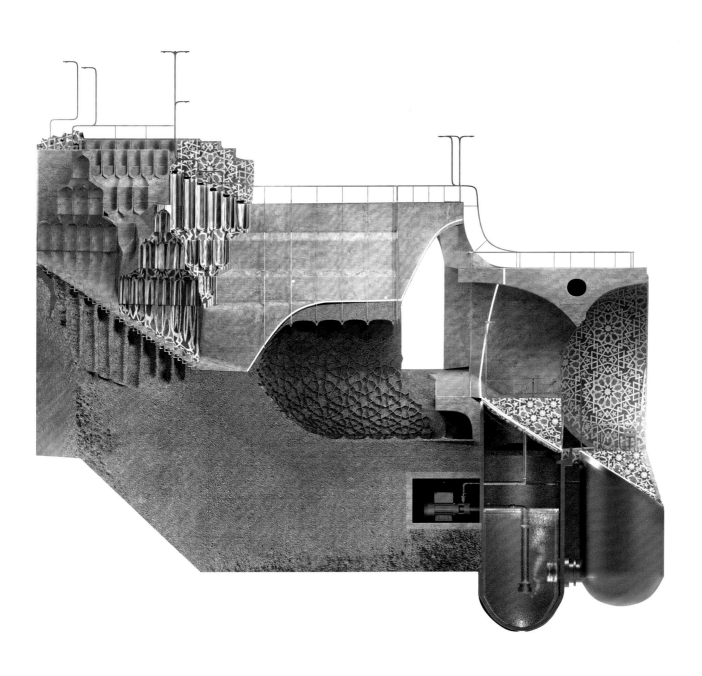

Yuanyi Zhou and Wenjia Go,
Oddkin Architecture Istanbul,
University of Pennsylvania
Weitzman School of Design,
Philadelphia, Pennsylvania,
2018

The Oddkin Architecture Istanbul studio was instructed
by Ferda Kolatan with Michael Zimmerman in the autumn
of 2018 and co-sponsored by the GAD Foundation
Istanbul. This partial section shows how water irrigation
infrastructure, soil enforcement, handrails, lighting fixtures,
arabesque tiling and concrete muqarnas all combine into
a new terracing architecture for the city's Sanatkarlar Park.

Oddly Familiar: A New Kind of Urban Architecture

The second project includes student samples from Oddkin Architecture Istanbul, a design research studio conducted at the University of Pennsylvania Weitzman School of Design. The titular term 'oddkin' was coined by Donna Haraway who defines it as 'beings requiring each other in unexpected collaborations and combinations'.[2] The studio examined how this curious neologism could inform new forms of urban architecture. The site is Istanbul, the historically rich and deeply layered Turkish megalopolis with an estimated 18 million inhabitants. Like many cities of similar size, culture and complexity, Istanbul's architecture is dominated by idiosyncratic accumulations of built matter. Building parts, infrastructural pieces, leftover green spaces, street furniture and forgotten historical monuments all mingle and amalgamate into concrete yet highly ambiguous urban artefacts. While these artefacts with their mixed-up character account for large portions of the city, we usually pay little attention to them, and if we do we treat them as undesirable residue to be cleaned up or demolished.

The oddkin concept encourages a paradigmatic change in the ways we view our environment and how we give meaning and value to the objects populating it. In response to the current environmental crisis and modernity's complicity in it, Haraway promotes an ecology of cross-categorical connectivity, unfamiliar kinship and strange hybridisations. While her ecology aims at the scale of the earth and beyond, useful parallels can be drawn regarding the architecture of cities. The residual aggregates described above are full of potential once we develop strategies to lift them from obscurity through new relational forms and acts of re-origination. To think and design along these lines means to innovate by utilising the immense repertoire of stuff that cities already contain, to register estranged objects, to borrow components and to articulate new coherences through which they can flourish

The Istanbul projects all depict Genuine Hybrids as composites, assembled mostly from urban artefacts that no longer possess a clear or traceable origin. Machinic parts mix with ornamentation and earth, traditional Ottoman patterns and colours seep into metro stations, and preciously tiled components form odd kinships with vacant basements. But none of these

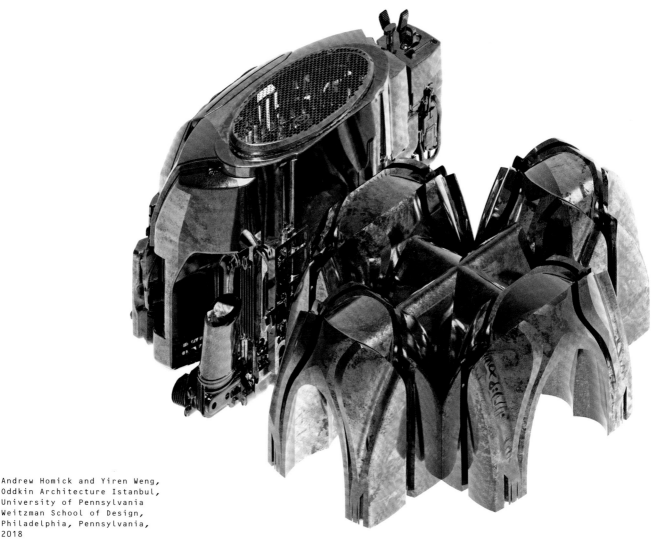

Andrew Homick and Yiren Weng,
Oddkin Architecture Istanbul,
University of Pennsylvania
Weitzman School of Design,
Philadelphia, Pennsylvania,
2018

Axonometric of a subterranean power station with a small built-in prayer chamber.

Andrew Homick and Yiren Weng,
Eddkin Architecture Istanbul,
University of Pennsylvania
Weitzman School of Design,
Philadelphia, Pennsylvania,
2018

A series of estranged architectural
components, ornamental features and other
details from existing Ottoman fountains,
kiosks and pavilions are brought together,
re-originating into a new Genuine Hybrid.

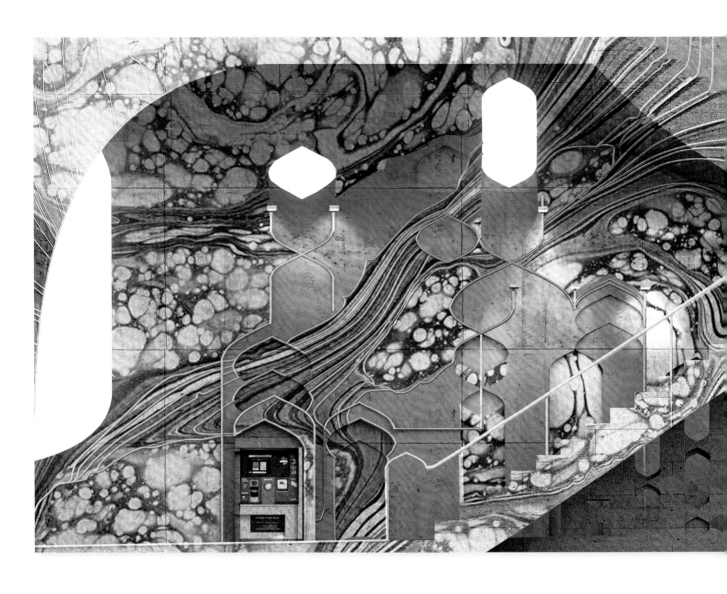

rla Bonilla,
dkin Architecture Istanbul,
iversity of Pennsylvania
itzman School of Design,
iladelphia, Pennsylvania,
18

ove: Elevation of a metro station interior.
concrete wall turns into a hybrid artefact
creating odd mixtures between mundane
ects such as handrails, electrical tubes,
nding machines and the traditional Turkish
form of Ebru painting.

hua Zhang,
dkin Architecture Istanbul,
iversity of Pennsylvania
itzman School of Design,
iladelphia, Pennsylvania,
18

oosite: Axonometric of a pavilion
signed by combining residual masonry
ces with traditional Islamic tiling and
n extrusions co-opted from the nearby
sretiye Mosque.

hybrid architectures are simple collages made haphazardly from found objects. In fact, all these combinations are initially triggered by affinities of some kind, like mutually relatable geometrical features, form, material, texture, colour and so forth. The assembled pieces of the hybrids are carefully, and collaboratively, attuned to each other, resulting in coherent but not necessarily harmonious architectural expressions. This is of particular significance as each one of these urban objects provides a unique experience for the observer by drawing from everyday local conditions and cultural memories alike without repressing the vital tensions and contradictory qualities so characteristic of Istanbul.

Purity and Hybridisation

The projects discussed above speculate on authentic hybrid entities that are freed from pure origins and express categorical difference and mixed heritages. But architecture of a mixed nature, ambiguous and noncommittal to a single source of origin, is of course not an invention of the digital era. Hybridity has been inseparably linked – as its counterpart – to an architecture of purity since the days of antiquity. At times the discipline strives for universal clarity in hope of conveying a definitive truth content; at times it channels its ambitions towards the messiness of locality, variability and stylistic eclecticism. These pure/hybrid fluctuations can be traced over millennia in the successive and cyclical play between so-called early and late phases of styles. When examining the 25-year history of digital architecture today, one cannot help but notice what appears to be yet another late-phase transition, this time reversing the pioneering principles of an earlier, more orthodox digitalism.

At the beginning of the digital era, in the 1990s, progressive architecture was predominantly characterised by a relatively homogeneous formalism. This grew largely out of newly accessible computational techniques that were inferred to be analogous to the generative processes in nature. The ensuing aesthetics of flows, particles, topological surfaces and self-similar repetition thus became synonymous with real material forces constituting nature itself. In the end the computation/nature analogy served to establish the most recent ideological brand of purity. And by representing the very qualities

of change, variability and adaptation as foundational elements of a dynamic nature, this ideology, paradoxically, reaffirmed once again a universal concept of origin from which architectural form derived and to which it was ultimately beholden.

During this early phase of the digital project, various software and fabrication packages drove progress and directly impacted how designers and fabricators worked. In contrast, social media's copy-based technologies were viewed as inconsequential to the operations of generating novel form, structure and geometry. Image-sharing technologies were initially seen as passive tools or mere distribution devices until their capacity to distort, reassemble and eventually conjure up whole new composite realities became an undeniable fact. This marks the pivotal moment where the digital moved from a purist narrative towards one of hybridisation.

Ultimately, all purist notions such as truth, nature or universality hinge on one fundamental prerequisite; that in architecture, and culture at large, exists a time- and place-independent quality able to resist change. Concepts of origin (and originality) are inseparably tied to this prerequisite, functioning much like an anchor resisting the pull of time. But given our own time with its diverse societal interests and microconstituents, its powerful technologies of reproduction, alteration and proliferation, such essentialist concepts and value systems have lost their validity. Instead we should aim for a different kind of ethic that calls for a more liberal, almost alchemical attitude towards concepts of origin, and conceives an architectural authenticity, digital or otherwise, that utilises hybrids as not only an inevitable, but also a desirable and fertile aspect of contemporary culture. ᴆ

Notes
1. Walter Benjamin, *Illuminations*, Schocken Books (New York), 1968, p 217.
2. Donna Haraway, *Staying with the Trouble: Making Kin in the Chthulucene*, Duke University Press (Durham, NC and London), 2016, p 4.

IMPACT
DISRUP

Hernán Díaz Alonso / HDA-X,
Bubbly Shoe with Fur,
2019

This variation of the Bubbly Shoe mixes
felt bubbles with tufts of realistic fur,
merging the abstract and literal.

GATHERED THOUGHTS OF

FUL TION

Hernán Díaz Alonso

A DISTRACTED MIND

Los Angeles architectural iconoclast **Hernán Díaz Alonso**, director of SCI-Arc and founder of HDA-X, conceives of the architectural profession as needing to constantly push the boundaries of form and space. It should forever be re-examining and disrupting itself. Here he uses the shoe industry as a microcosm for this process of re-evaluation and conceptual crossover.

Architecture always seems to be in crisis. Today the crisis is figuring out how to define its impact. The discipline, like others including art, music and film, has been affected by the development of new technologies and by a series of cultural changes. The impact of digital proliferation is still being discussed some 30 years later, mainly because the terms of engagement are still being defined through the canonic traditions of architecture. Buildings remain at the centre of the architectural conversation, but the building industry directly contributes to the devaluation of the building itself as a cultural force, not necessarily as a tool for financial influence or 'progress'.

Smash

Architecture is visibly changing as architectural concept thinking is becoming more and more a way to see, understand and operate in an ever-changing world. As an overall strategy, the discipline of architecture should always be in a state of re-examination, including, but not limited to, how the concept of architectural thinking can be applied to architecture itself, cities, society and culture at large. As an extension of this interest, it is necessary to focus more specifically on the degree to which architecture and design could be interpreted as an accumulative mutation of interactions, or as having new potential for integration.

Architecture is and should remain an existential problem, the question being: can architecture redefine existence in a literal sense? It must stay a humanist problem, as well as reclaim an artistic proposition.

Jolt

Living in an era of images and effects, we easily confuse fiction with reality (or reality as a fiction). The most impactful element of this state of things is that architecture is a way to operate and think about the world as expanding beyond buildings. There is a huge amount of opportunity in creating new platforms of engagement and operation and we must understand this relationship.

Architecture at the end of the day can only express the culture of now. Like science, fiction is never really about the future, but is only a myopic view of the present. Architecture can similarly only operate at such a limited level.

Forces of creativity and imagination within architecture are currently undergoing a massive shift, becoming much more collaborative than ever before – but not in a multidisciplinary sense. Architecture is already multidisciplinary, as it constantly borrows from other disciplines. In response, different models and modes of practice will emerge that are not presently imaginable. The next 20 years will be defined by computer science, mathematics and liberal arts, among which architecture arguably finds itself.

lash

rchitects, unlike those in any other field, are in a ermanent state of engagement, and must therefore e strategic in how to capitalise on this within a model of practice – whether as a business or vehicle or innovation.

Architects are specialists in being generalists. They must first figure out how to build relevance through disruption in order to transcend the limitations associated with these categories of approach. Disruption is cool and crucial, more so than are peculation and innovation. As in any pursuit, success as a price, which is the fear of failing. What makes someone 'successful' can be the same elements contributing to fear of failure. The only way to assuage is fear as an architect is to dismantle and rebuild, dismantle and rebuild, dismantle and rebuild, until the ocus of importance lies in the process itself rather than the result. This is not easy to do because architecture subjective. If one's occupation is to generate research with the aim of curing cancer, one either cures cancer r does not. How does an architect know if his or her m has been fulfilled in the same way? How does one measure whether architecture is successful in its mission? What should the system of measurement even be?

Therefore, disruption is important. Because often, the same drives that generate progress can also act as n impediment to it.

Take shoe designs as an example. Sports shoes re becoming fashion shoes, and fashion shoes are replicating the techniques and technologies of sports shoes. Since fashion produces some of the fastest

design changes, it is a good place to provoke and be disruptive. Shoes are typological. In architecture, one should challenge typology and move away from it. With a shoe, you are limited by the function of the feet. But you can challenge by layering or aggregating materials for effect over an existing typology.

Narrative and exaggeration guide the design of HDA-X's footwear range. The HDA-X Haircut Shoe is covered with fur and long hair that is designed to be cut, groomed and styled, giving a sports shoe individuality. The Inflatable Skin Shoe has bubbles of air to give a sense of weightlessness, and the design of the Bubbly Shoe provokes ideas of exaggeration by covering the entire shoe in bubbles, removing performance qualities in favour of an aesthetic statement. The shoes are constituted using recycled materials, synthetic furs, felts and transparent recycled plastics. Mistakes are always embraced in the design process, and in the shoe range the user can alter the shoe's form by cutting the hair, in effect individualising each shoe. The user may make a mistake, revealing the scalp below. The scalp in this case is also designed. This method reshapes customisation, taking it to a different level than is currently available in shoe design.

Hernán Díaz Alonso / HDA-X,
Haircut Shoe,
2019

The Haircut footwear range arrive covered
in fur with matching bubbly scissors
that can be used to groom and sculpt a
custom shoe.

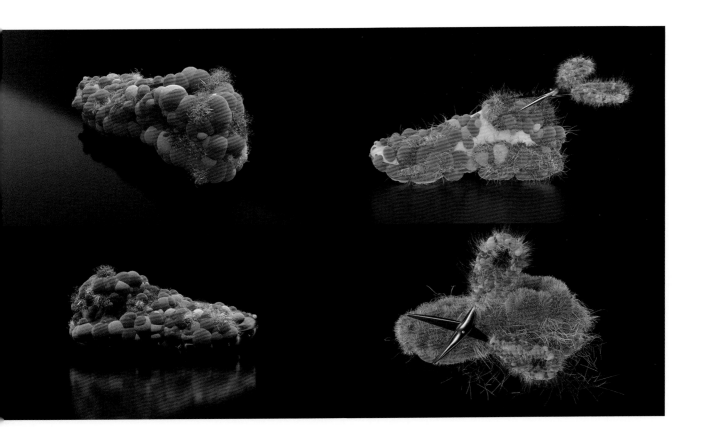

ernán Díaz Alonso / HDA-X,
nflatable Shoe,
019

ne most transparent of the collection,
e Inflatable Shoe is filled with air and
flates or deflates according to the
dividual shape of its wearer's foot.

Bounce

Architectural thinking may represent the future of practice, the future of the world, an alternate future of either, a new possible future (perhaps best to be avoided), a false start, or a truly terrible idea that refuses to die. The future impact of the field should encompass the moment of contamination when a freshly minted paradigm finally becomes identifiable in the act of its alteration into something new and as yet unidentifiable – a sampling of the orphaned drafts for what might still turn out to be a successful mutation.

Simply, disruption is a contaminant. The process of disruption will contaminate further contaminations with an alien technical logic, producing subsequent mutations and intimating evolution as a stage rehearsal – unpolished, invisible, in process – and normally not meant to be seen. Here we should exploit contemporary models of artificial intelligence to produce continuously evolving architectural disruptions, where two conflicting models are locked in a continuous game of comprehension and generation.

Hernán Díaz Alonso / HDA-X,
Haircut Shoe,
2018

The shoe is unboxed with long synthetic hair designed to be groomed, shaved, styled and recycled by its wearer.

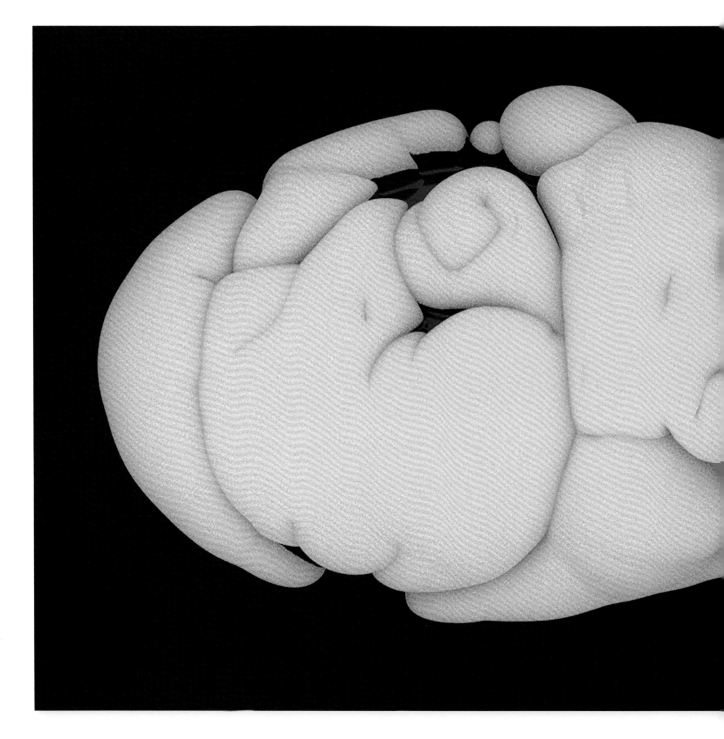

The hope is to catch a fleeting glimpse of evolutionary outcomes stranger than anyone could expect

Hernán Díaz Alonso / HDA-X,
Inflatable Skin Shoe,
2018

In this variation, the material is designed
to act as a second skin, augmenting
and adapting to individual foot shapes
or defects.

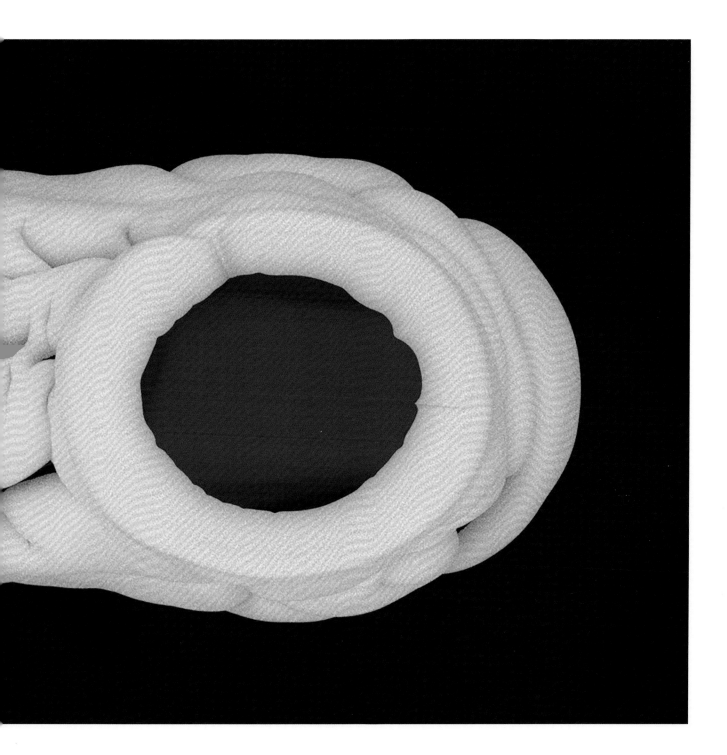

The first model, the current state of design, is somehow to read and understand architectural intention purely through the image. This model will evolve the ability of nonhuman systems to find novel commonalities or architectural classifications between disparate design projects. This happens through direct formal analysis and, thus, in the systematic absence of traditional theoretical discourse. The second form of disruption in architecture should leverage the synthesised agendas of the first to generate new architectural provocations and imagery. In short, the first understands, the second designs.

The idea of disruption – or architectural thinking as proxy, in a way – represents a radical set of unresolved and dissimilar contaminations of accepted practice that will themselves become contaminated. Through the diffuse implementation of multiple instances of cross-disciplinary technical language, like that describing AI and technology of which we are not yet aware, the hope is to catch a fleeting glimpse of evolutionary outcomes stranger than anyone could expect. Indifferent to our desires and far from eugenic fantasy, the product is neither of adaptation nor of intelligent design; a beast, but ideally and after many failures, in some sense, life. ⌂

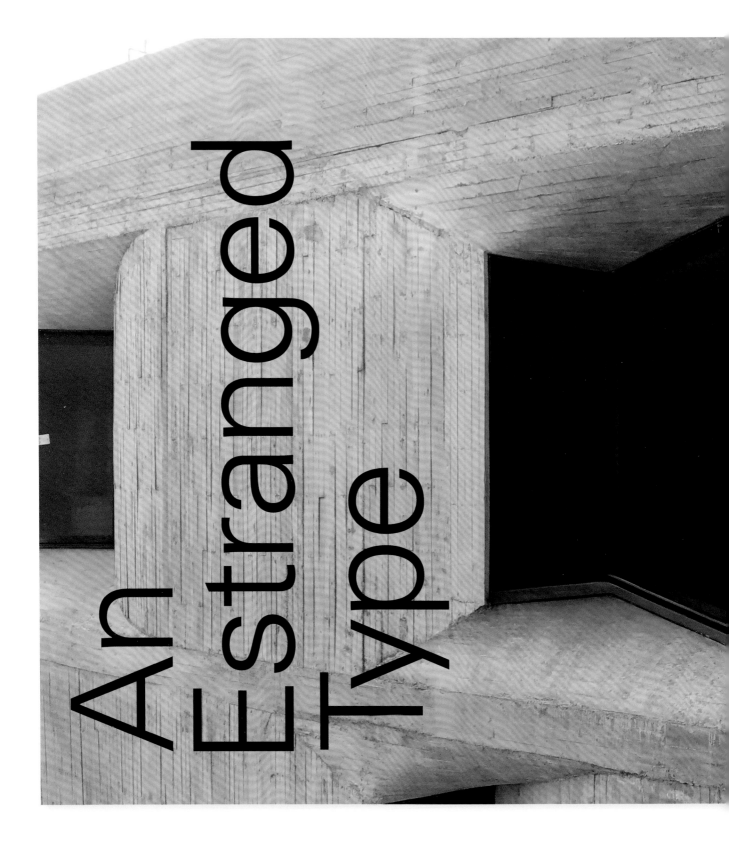

An Estranged Type

Founding partner of New York-based Young & Ayata and tutor at the University of Pennsylvania Weitzman School of Design and Pratt Institute, **Kutan Ayata** describes DL 1310, a residential project in Mexico, the formal innovation of which was confined to a metre-wide, concrete facade wrap due to the constricted nature of the site. It is the choreography of the wrap and its window apertures, and the fabrication techniques used in its making, that give the building its unique presence.

Old Techniques, Familiar Materials and Peculiar Outcomes

Young & Ayata with Michan Architecture,
DL 1310 apartments,
Mexico City,
2020

One of the large trapezoidal windows with its dark-grey
tinted glass. The ruled surface doubles as reflection as the
aperture appears to be further deepening.

The range of precision in architectural construction can oscillate between the clinical operations of a robotic arm and the unpredictability of a human arm. It simply depends on project resources. Not every project reaps from the budgets that can fund the latest technological fabrication tools with the capacity to deposit the right material to the right position in space without human interpretation, mediating digital input directly into material reality. In fact, the vast majority of building output in the world is subject to low budget margins that require conventional and manual construction techniques. DL 1310, a collaborative project between Young & Ayata and Michan Architecture, operates through similar constraints.

DL 1310 is a four-storey, mid-market speculative residential building with seven units, located in the southwestern part of Mexico City in a developing middle-class neighbourhood. This type of market-driven development generally allows little room for experimentation, especially in the planimetric articulation of the project, leaving only the slightest of possibilities to 'compose' windows in a maybe interesting manner. This project threrefore hedged all its expressive potential and architectural discovery into a 90-centimetre (approximately 3-foot) zone around its perimeter, by imagining how the notion of typical aperture could be reinterpreted towards an effect of estrangement. The plan is thus all it can be within the restricted footprint and does not have any ambition to redefine the typology within the conditions of its layout. The hope, however, was that the effect of the aperture design would resonate deeper into the building, altering the sense of spatiality held within a normative floor plan.

The project is situated on a very narrow street, and the site is relatively deep in relation to its street frontage. The typical strategy of 'building to plot lines' on the sides as permitted by the zoning ordinance has not been utilised in favour of having a standalone building volume, simply a box. It has 3-metre (10-foot) setbacks on the sides and back, while it sits flush on the street front. There is a stack of four two-bedroom apartments facing the back side (south) towards a lower valley with open views, while the front consists of one three-bedroom duplex and two one-bedrooms facing the street. The building's envelope is cast-in-situ steel-reinforced concrete. It also performs in its structural capacity. Since Mexico City's climate allows a looser definition between interior and exterior, the envelope does not require the two environments to be thermally insulated and separated. This results in minimal deployment of building materials, so performance is not reliant on technical complexity: it uses basic steel mullion profiles and single-pane glass, and no cavity/layering is required to provide sufficient environmental comfort solutions.

Off-the-Surface Apertures
The most significant design decision defining the character of the project, both inside and outside, is the articulation of the apertures. The inward pivoting of the rectangular operable windows away from the building's

Street-level view rendering.

The most significant design decision defining the character of the project, both inside and outside, is the articulation of the apertures

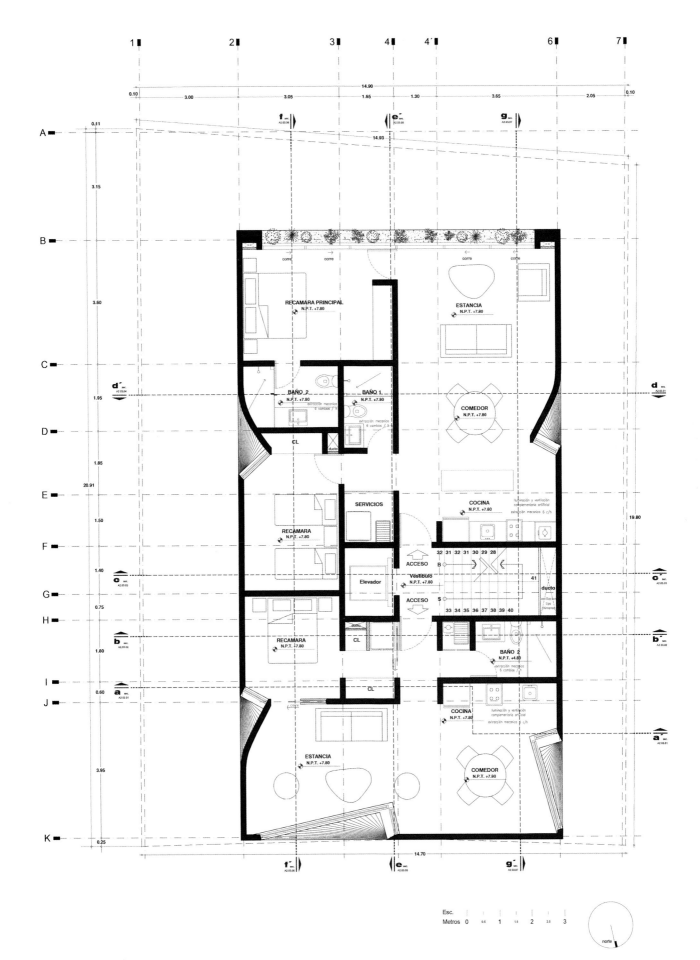

Floor plan of the second and third levels
showing the shift of the apertures that in turn
create variation of units from floor to floor.

Esc.
Metros 0   0.5   1   1.5   2   2.5   3

norte

61

planar surface results in three other surfaces that ensure the continuity of enclosure. Two of these define identical ruled surface geometries to negotiate the planimetric rotation of the windows between the horizontal slab edges. The third is a vertical surface, conceived either as a planar trapezoidal window or as a curved concrete extrusion. The module consisting of the trapezoidal window with its operable partner occurs on the street facade, articulating large openings and turning of the corners. The other unit, comprising an operable window and concrete surfaces, articulates oblique apertures on the side facades enabling the more private spaces of the apartments to turn away from adjacent buildings and orient themselves towards either the front or back with open views.

Modes of Concrete

Several material articulations were crucial in rendering the character of the building. The first is the way in which the concrete surface is engraved horizontally and vertically with specific effects to break down the perception of its initial monolithic appearance. The slab-edge surfaces, as well as the ruled surfaces below and above the windows, are articulated with horizontally inscribed lines to unify them towards the effect of local thickening of the slabs. All other vertical wall instances are articulated with vertically inscribed lines on the concrete, breaking down the building into slabs and walls, distinctly registering each floor. This helps to conceal the cold joints stemming out of the pour sequence of concrete, but most importantly enables an alternate reading of the typical registration of slab-edges as an unlevelled condition around the building.

Left: the aperture that receives the trapezoidal window along with the operable rectangular window.

Right: the aperture that receives only the operable rectangular window.

Looking up the east facade reveals the directional shifts of the timber-board patterns on concrete.

Woodiness of Wood Versus Woodiness of Fibreglass

The traditional and time-honoured method of formwork in Mexico is timber boards. There are several common approaches affiliated with timber formwork, the most indulged of which is the registration of the wood grain onto the concrete surface. This is a phenomenon where each grain field raises and reacts slightly differently against the moisture of the concrete and subsequently grafts its surface pattern onto it. In other words, the 'natural woodiness' of the formwork registers onto the exterior surface of the cured mix of tricalcium silicate, dicalcium silicate, tricalcium aluminate, and a tetra-calcium aluminoferrite (concrete mix). In DL 1310, this operates in two different directions.

In the case of the ruled surfaces, of which there are five different sizes, a reusable mould was deployed. A single mould could be used for the ruled surfaces both below and above the trapezoidal windows. While the lower ruled surface is integrated with the slab cast below like an upstand beam, the upper ruled surface is cast together with the slab above as an integral downstand beam. A timber mould was not an option as it would be impossible to take out without breaking the sharp edges around the cast concrete, and it also would not be possible to reuse, as the surface would deteriorate after casting. The challenge here was therefore the need to produce the surface registration of timber boards to maintain consistency with the way the slab edges would be cast. For this, fibreglass was utilised. The five ruled surface instances were fabricated out of timber as 'positives'. These were then used as moulds to fabricate the 'negative' fibreglass moulds that registered the texture of the timber boards. These moulds were flexible so could be bent out of shape to release after the casting. They were also very lightweight, allowing ease of handling for the workers. In the case of the vertical surfaces, the boards change direction and character. To reinforce a subtle shift in texture and a very slight relief in surface, tiny shims were used at random locations at the rear of the shuttering to push each of the boards out of plane. This resulted in a concrete surface that developed an amplified texture and shadow lines along the seams of the vertical boards. Additionally, the concrete surface not only registered the grain, but also the presence of the individual timber boards that cast the concrete walls.

Glass as Surface and Window as Object

The last important material decision that has a significant impact on the project is the dark-grey tint of the glass. This too performs in two different ways: from outside, the opacity of the dark glass reinforces the monolithic quality of the mass; and through its reflectivity it re-registers the ruled surface, further deepening the condition of the apertures. As one moves inside, the properties of the tinted glass evolve. When the trapezoidal window is in the frontal position, the backlighting and lip detail in the back of the ruled surfaces render the frame of the window as well as the glass barely visible to the naked eye. In turn, the oblique

The interior view of the trapezoidal window shows the window frame completely disappear behind the lip in the base and header, staging the operable rectangular window as a severed object in space.

view of the small operable window now sitting in the room as a severed object creates a curious condition whereby one contemplates how to look out of the 'window'.

Aesthetic Impact

The DL 1310 project is an exercise where two very familiar construction materials take on specific articulations with multiple readings towards an affect that challenges assumptions regarding the aesthetics of residential typology and the basic architectural element of the window. All along the design effort has been about defining an ambiguous architectural object that neither expresses its organisation nor its programme, but instead its own physical manifestation. New mediation technologies pave the way for the exploration of emergent concepts, but this by itself does not guarantee a fundamentally strong exploration of novelty. It should be clear by now, especially after the last 30 years of digital exploration, that if the pursuit of novelty strictly foregrounds the aesthetic expression of the most advanced technological interface of the day, such an outcome will be consumed at the rate of the ever-accelerating technological innovation cycles. It seems clear that new design and construction technologies alone are simply not enough to build a strong discourse. An agenda beyond new means and methods is crucial. For Young & Ayata, this is the exploration of aesthetics of estrangement. ∆

Text © 2020 John Wiley & Sons Ltd.
Images courtesy of Young & Ayata / Michan Architecture

The Impact of Automobile Design on Architecture

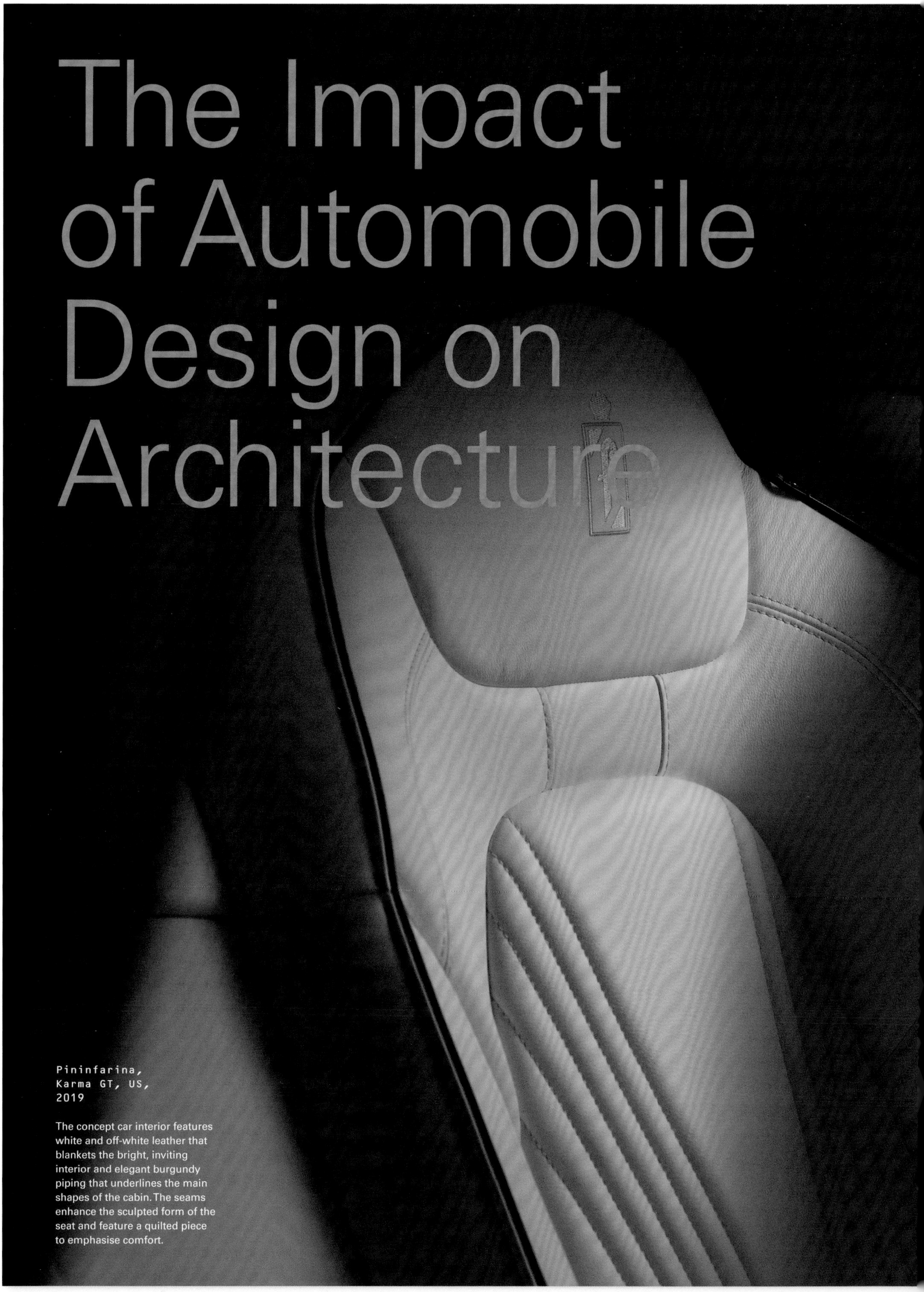

Pininfarina,
Karma GT, US,
2019

The concept car interior features white and off-white leather that blankets the bright, inviting interior and elegant burgundy piping that underlines the main shapes of the cabin. The seams enhance the sculpted form of the seat and feature a quilted piece to emphasise comfort.

Paolo Pininfarina
and Paolo Trevisan

ininfarina,
yrela residential
ower block,
āo Paulo, Brazil,
014

he building's use of metal
tructures creates a curvature
nat makes the residential
ower seem as though it
/ere sculpted by the power
f the wind.

Paolo Pininfarina, chairman of longstanding Italian car designer and maker Pininfarina, and **Paolo Trevisan**, Head of Design and Architecture at Pininfarina of America, describe how the seamless, double-curved formal transitions made in automobile design can be transferable to architecture, and question the discrete separateness of building elements and techniques, for example roofs and walls, as illustrated by their Cyrela residential tower block in São Paulo.

Battista 'Pinin' Farina ('Pinin' being his Piedmontese nickname as the youngest son of the family) founded the automobile design company Carrozzeria Pininfarina in Turin in 1930, initially to build special car bodies for individual customers or for small production runs. Having become known for its unique aesthetic, over the decades it has designed and manufactured auto bodies for Ferrari, Alfa Romeo, Cadillac and Volvo, among others. In the 1980s, Battista's son Sergio understood that the brand had potential beyond the original automotive sector and believed that, step by step, Pininfarina could become a 360-degree design house. What followed was a gradual process of diversification into industrial and furniture design and, in 2013, into architecture under the leadership of Battista's grandson, Paolo Pininfarina (this having become the family's official surname in 1961). The firm carries into its later endeavours the styling it made famous in the automobile business.

Early on, Battista Farina and Enzo Ferrari made one-off racing cars – technical and precise, but noisy and dirty. In 1938 Ferrari needed financing for its racing car La Scuderia, so Pininfarina designers turned his automobile into a piece of art for gentlemen drivers. It became the new standard for luxury car design and eventually came to define Ferrari's renowned brand. This is what Pininfarina is doing today with architecture and design in the built environment: creating 'one-off' pieces of art, and prioritising 'una bella carrozzeria' or 'a nice bodywork'.

Pininfarina,
Karma GT, US,
2019

below: The design philosophy is fluid through the vehicle's emotionally driven lines, with all-new body sides, an aggressive front and contrasting black roof, transforming the Revero GT's character into a bespoke vehicle that blends Californian innovation with traditional Italian sports car style.

opposite: The Karma GT unites the two brands through shared commitment to high design.

Automotive Heritage

Much like the ever-changing technology of the car manufacturing industry, the approach of architecture is changing. A building is no longer perceived as the simple sum of its parts – a roof plus walls plus windows. This is typical with A-Class surface design in the automotive industry, but it is quite new for building geometry. As an auto designer, Pininfarina contributed to both a cultural and visual movement. The cars Pininfarina designs are not only purchased and used all over the world, but their image is widely published, and shapes the perception of contemporary aesthetics. This cultural influence is on a scale that architecture does not regularly achieve. In transferring the company's automotive design to the design of buildings, Pininfarina is looking to innovate the architecture industry and make a cultural impact.

The car has always been one of the most complex objects ever created. The last few decades have seen an increased complexity in buildings as well – they now integrate several advanced technologies, mostly related to building systems (eg heating, cooling, lighting) as well as accessibility and interacting with the occupants. These buildings are transforming into living environments, complex machines: they are becoming cars, but they are not yet like cars in scale.

To make a scalable model, all parties involved need to agree on the standard by which they are measuring the scale. This will determine the tests that will be run, which will in turn optimise the design process to satisfy cost and quality standards. Design standards have been reached in the automobile industry for electrical vehicles and their operating systems. In regard to the construction industry, we are not quite there yet. For example, the building industry's scale is determined by repetition of elements such as the standardised prefabricated panels one finds in hospitals and hotels. Aside from this repetition, no other standard has been as widely implemented in the building industry.

Automobile design is not easily scalable to buildings. The auto industry employs robotics and other direct manufacturing methods which allow for a high degree of precision and a final product close to the original design intention. The process of design to construction in the building industry, on the other hand, relies on losing information from its inception to construction. The designer has precise control over the conceptual design when working in the 3D modelling software, but as the model incorporates more and more information from consultants and contractors, intentions are compromised in the process of translation.

Even in building design however, software has become more and more sophisticated, as is the full manufacturing process of automation. New technology reduces risks and extra costs associated with human error, and allows more attention to environmental considerations. 'Robots' have made this possible. New technology has changed the way we design – not only because automation allows us to replicate the fabrication of an object, but also because it allows us to design a full experience for the user. Artificial intelligence can understand us intimately. With a car or a building, the end-user's needs are dynamic, and as buildings and spaces evolve with the design process the user remains at the centre of all decision-making, extending beyond merely responding to physical needs. Whether residential, corporate, hospitality or simply masterplanning projects, purity, elegance and innovation drive the human-centric design process and aesthetic.

There is great potential for disciplinary innovation in architecture, such as discovering ways to bring quality and time control of the manufacturing process to architecture. For instance, rapid prototyping and off-site construction are becoming more and more present in architecture, not only within the design process, but also in the construction phase. Indeed, car manufacturing technologies will soon influence the planning, design, fabrication and assembly of building elements through an integrated supply chain optimisation strategy.

Marriage of Functionality and Design

A saying at Pininfarina is, 'You fall in love with the exterior and then you live with the interior.' The interior i infinitely more complex given the ergonomic constraints not to mention the variety of functions that need to be addressed. The interior is a living environment, and it is innately human – often defined by the tastes and habits of the buyer. These complexities and intricacies have made purchasing a Pininfarina-designed car in a super-premium market so exclusive.

It is in the details as well that Pininfarina's history of automobile design has influenced the architectural product. Curvilinear silhouettes speak to that inspiration The Bobič & Marmor yacht interior shown at the 2017 Monaco Yacht Show demonstrated that, through advanced milling technologies, design can mirror the complexity of the car body with natural, warm materials In this case, wood shaped by master carpenters from

Pininfarina,
Bobič & Marmor yacht interior,
Monaco,
2017

above: Unveiled at the Monaco Yacht Show, this space blends two noble materials – wood and stone – to create an extraordinary, immersive cocoon experience for visitors. The joints in the material create contrast features in the ceiling.

below: The elegance of the stone welcomes visitors at the entrance and melts into the wood to invite guests further within. Walls in fluid forms lead to the heart of the space which is a sculptural desk made of stone and wood.

Pininfarina,
Cyrela residential tower block,
São Paulo, Brazil,
2014

The building is inspired by curves and shapes that convey movement and dynamism, characteristics of a major metropolis, while the details highlight the form of the building.

he joinery and furniture-making company Bobič
Yacht Interior and stone crafted by the firm of Marmor
Hotavlje, both based in Slovenia, were balanced by
Pininfarina using technological software, inventively
marrying the use of digital tools to hand-craftsmanship.

Cyrela by Pininfarina, a residential tower in
sophisticated São Paulo, Brazil, was designed in 2014 by
Pininfarina for the developer Cyrela. A luxury property
with dynamic automotive lines, the tower exemplifies
the forward movement of this exciting city. Its curving
symmetry gives all sides equal emphasis, negating
the idea of a front or rear face to the building. The
balconies at each level follow the structure's curvature.
Battista Pininfarina once found design inspiration in
the wind-sculpted snow banks on the side of the road.
Like the streamlined automobiles that sprang from that
inspiration, the Cyrela building too suggests that it has
been shaped by the wind.

Human-Centric Design

Pininfarina's sleek, Italian aesthetic is rooted in a design
language that accentuates the flow and movement
of lines – forming a timeless silhouette native to its
architectural practice. The firm's vision seeks to transmit
emotion through subtly elevating the essential human
experience, from activities that span driving a car to
relaxing at home. It is this commitment to elegant living,
hallmarked by a distinct functionality of design, that
accounts for Pininfarina's special attention to the spatial
elements of architecture – a priority that hails from a
distinctive, automotive heritage. Ultimately, Pininfarina's
approach puts the end user at the heart of a uniquely
human-centric design process. ⌂

THE MEGA-VOID

Patrik Schumacher

UNLEASHING THE COMMUNICATIVE IMPACT OF TALL BUILDINGS

Zaha Hadid Architects,
Tai Kang Headquarters,
Wuhan, China,
due for completion 2022

The dramatic spectacle of this interior urbanism delivers a thrilling sensation. But this sensation makes productive sense. The visceral attraction is signalling the anticipated richness of productive encounters.

On a whistle-stop tour of some of Zaha Hadid Architects' skyscrapers around the world, principal **Patrik Schumacher** describes how the typology and philosophy behind high-rise towers needs to change. Currently most towers have segmented, separated, sealed, blind-to-one-another floors. He argues for an architecture that, like cathedrals, takes the viewer's mind soaring upwards, urges designers to encourage roaming, and speculates on the emergence of 'interior urbanism' in respect to these buildings.

Zaha Hadid Architects, Leeza SOHO Tower, Beijing, China, 2019

The mega-void cuts right through the tower in a continuous spiralling move that opens the tower to its urban context. The smooth trajectory of the void is punctuated by big trusses that stitch the two slices together.

The digital design tools that have become available to the discipline of architecture since the 1990s were congenial to its concurrent pursuit of complexity and empowered radically new concepts and sensibilities that ushered in the movement and style of Parametricism. Twenty-five years later architects are impacting at scale, across all project types. The high-rise typology was the most resistant and last to open up to the impact of the new complexity and dynamism demanded and delivered by the digital revolution.

Historical Context, Task and Opportunity

We are living in an era of unprecedented urban concentration. Contemporary urban life is becoming ever more complex, with diverse overlapping audiences browsing through many simultaneous urban amenities. A dense proximity of complementary social offerings, and a new intensity of communication across different activities, distinguish contemporary life from the modern period of separation and repetition. Such a network of activities can evolve bottom up in an urban texture that offers the spatial connective freedom of urban channels and voids. What would it take to continue such an evolving synergetic urbanity within a building?

The skyscraper seems locked in the Fordist paradigm of segregating segmentation and serial repetition. The tower typology is the last bastion of this bygone era, and has so far resisted the injection of any significant measure of spatial complexity. Towers are still driven by pure quantity. Their volume is generally generated by pure extrusion and their inner space is nothing but the multiplication of identical floor plates. They are vertical dead-end corridors, usually cut off from the ground plane by a podium. All this is so for seemingly good economic reasons. However, this economy, an economy of costs rather than benefits, is increasingly dubious.

The skyscraper's organisational structure is too simple and too constricting. Towers are hermetic units, which are themselves arrays of equally hermetic units (floors). This feature of strict segmentation with its characteristic poverty of connectivity is antithetical to contemporary work patterns and business relations as well as to contemporary urban life in general. The time is ripe to challenge the standard tower typology and demand that it too participate in the general societal restructuring from Fordism to post-Fordism.

Post-Fordist Costs and Benefits

The usual tower typology stacks up floors that remain blind to each other. Due to the normally centrally located core, the usable surfaces on each floor are also highly segregated. Towers are generally big investments and economic pressures are brought to bear, demanding cost-efficiency. But costs are only one side of an economic appraisal. A proper appraisal includes both costs and benefits in a cost–benefit analysis. The problem is that the benefit of providing floor surface is obvious and its measurement is trivial, while the appraisal of the benefits of navigability, inter-visibility and inter-awareness afforded by voids is not so trivial, cannot be as easily measured, and might therefore be overlooked. What is required here is entrepreneurial market leadership based on the intuition that the intuitive appeal of spaces with superb visual connectivity will draw in clients who are willing to pay the extra costs and more.

The idea could not be simpler: all buildings, especially towers, must become to a large extent empty, hollow, ie we must substitute usable floor surface with voids that afford deeply penetrating internal vistas.

We can have confidence that this will succeed within our contemporary knowledge economy with creative industry firms. Here real-estate costs are only a small fraction of human capital costs, and the prospect of increasing creative-knowledge worker productivity will be very much worth the expense of cutting voids into the dense packing of floors and desks. Visual density is more important than physical density, because it facilitates density of communication. This is not only a matter of facilitating actual encounters, conversations, exchanges and collaborations but works already via the thrill and stimulation of being viscerally immersed within a cluster of creatives. This sense of stimulation has its own intuitive rationality: the prospect of encounters, of learning opportunities, of collaborative ventures – all productivity- and thus life-enhancing – attracts those who are eager to thrive professionally.

What is the point of agglomerating thousands of people within a headquarters tower, if not the facilitation of cooperation, planned and unplanned? Post-Fordism implies that workers are no longer chained rigidly into an assembly line. Production is automated via reprogrammable robotic systems. This new technological era ushered in by the combustive combination of computation and networking, and now further enhanced via AI, has an enormously expanded capacity to absorb innovations. Production robots can be reprogrammed just in time and new service apps uploaded to billions at all times. The same applies to software updates. The Fordist mechanical assembly lines had very little ability to take on product innovations on the fly. Here cycles of innovation were counted in years or decades rather than months and weeks. In any case, the workers were still locked into the assembly chain as well. In contrast, all work is now able to focus on continuous innovation: research and development, marketing, financing. As workers become creative-knowledge workers they must become self-directed nodes in a continuous process of network self-organisation. There is no way that this can be planned from above. The leadership is busy building open platforms that might allow this self-organisation to flourish. Buildings are one important

type of platform that can make a difference. The costs of creating or renting these spatial communication platforms dwarf in comparison to the costs of the human capital that fills these buildings. A building that wastes and stunts this human capital is damaging the economy irrespective of its own construction costs. All the ideas, innovations and productive collaborations that might have been the result of bringing thousands of smart people into a volume, are the invisible opportunity cost that are missing from the calculations of each project budget. However, comparative analyses on the urban scale have demonstrated what urban economists call agglomeration economies.

Interior Urbanism and Unleashed Navigation
The idea of explicitly introducing navigation as a key agenda to be considered in the design of towers goes hand in hand with the attempt to inject a certain measure of differentiation and complexity into the vertical trajectory of the tower. The repetition of the same does not require a special design effort to facilitate orientation. And usually the navigation of towers is dead simple: just step into the elevator and select the required floor. As the complexity of the tower increases and public functions start to penetrate the tower, navigation becomes an issue. Navigation means much more than mere mechanical circulation. Navigation is the perceptual and conceptual penetration of a deep space. A legibly configured navigation space is called for that affords a certain visual penetration and mental map. Floors are no longer segregated black boxes. Such a space invites roaming rather than merely the seeking out of a pre-planned, known destination. While maintaining a strong sense of orientation, a strategic browsing should be made possible, affording unplanned but non-random

Zaha Hadid Architects,
Leeza SOHO Tower,
Beijing, China,
2019

right: Parametricism has matured and is delivering sophisticated state-of-the-art products at scale. This tower offers collaborative office space for hundreds of small and medium-sized enterprises gathered around the world's tallest atrium.

opposite: The void reveals to each floor what goes on on many more floors, above and below, inspiring interawareness as a first step to productive social interaction. It also provides awareness of the urban life beyond.

encounters, just like in a buzzing city fabric. This is the idea of 'interior urbanism'. The question is: Can the idea of interior urbanism be applied to towers? One solution is the idea of the mega-atrium, the tower as continuous void that can bring thousands of potentially inter-relevant activities into mutual view. An example of this is Zaha Hadid Architects' headquarters design for the Tai Kang Conglomerate in Wuhan, China (begun 2016, due for completion 2022).

These spaces express and facilitate the complexity, dynamism and communicative intensification of urban life in our 21st-century network society. Buildings must become porous and urbanised on the inside, allowing for increasing inter-visibility between the diverse social activities brought together, to maximise colocation synergies and to facilitate a browsing navigation. Another example of this is Zaha Hadid Architects' Dominion Tower in Moscow (2015) where a synergy cluster of creative-industry firms have naturally found each other.

The motivation to move into ever-larger, ever-denser cities, and into ever-larger buildings, is clear: we come together to network, to synergise knowledge, to exchange and to cooperate. The built environment becomes an information-rich, empowering and exhilarating 360-degree interface of communication and networking machine. However, it thereby also becomes an experience machine. Lose yourself and discover yourself!

The taller the tower, the more important becomes its mode of interfacing with the ground-plane. The large amount of traffic coming down from the tower usually occasions special spatial provisions on the ground floor. For instance, in the case of a hotel tower all additional facilities like lobbies, restaurants, bars, retail etc are located on the ground floor or near to the ground. Tall residential towers, as well as office towers, also demand ground-level expansion. Usually these additional space requirements are catered for by means of discrete podium blocks that separate the shaft of the tower from the ground. One of our key ambitions has been to find convincing alternatives to the 'tower on podium' typology, alternatives that avoid the intervention of a discrete third element between the ground surface and the tower itself. One such strategy is the sunken retail podium, as executed in Zaha Hadid Architects' Leeza SOHO tower in Beijing (2019).

The agendas of differentiation, interface and navigation combine to articulate a new paradigm for the design of complex towers in urban contexts. On this new basis the tower typology will receive a new lease of life in the central metropolitan societies, where the desire for connectivity (rather than pure quantity) drives urban density. In the future, even more than is evident already now, this super-dense build-up will be a mixed-use build-up, where multiple life processes intersect. These life processes need to be ordered in intricate ways that nevertheless remain legible. More than ever, the task of architectural design will be about the transparent articulation of relations for the sake of orientation and communication. Differentiation, interfacing and navigation are joined in a clear agenda that will require

Zaha Hadid Architects,
Tai Kang Headquarters,
Wuhan, China,
due for completion 2022

The massive void of the mega-atrium gathers the many firms of the conglomerate, plus retail spaces and a small business hotel. This is a 21st-century city square, a truly urban interior.

Zaha Hadid Architects,
Atrium, Morpheus,
Macau, China,
2019

Morpheus sports an exoskeleton that gives ample freedom to the complex atrium unfolding inside. This vertiginous space of flying can be traversed via 180-degree glazed panoramic elevators. The void is traversed by bridges that host social spaces like cafes and restaurants. Vistas open out also into the urban context.

he voids which are strung along the vertical axis might fuse into a mega-atrium that also affords panoramic elevators

aha Hadid Architects,
trium, Dominion Tower,
oscow, Russia,
015

is office tower in Moscow became a cluster of related eative industry firms who all guessed right that this space ould attract like-minded firms. Natural light, inter-visibility d shared social spaces create a fertile networking hub.

a sophisticated, versatile language of architecture. An expressed contemporary structure, like an optimised exoskeleton, helps naturally to differentiate the tower along its vertical axis. The exoskeleton also takes pressure off the core and allows more freedom for interior voiding. The voids which are strung along the vertical axis might fuse into a mega-atrium that also affords panoramic elevators to fly through a navigation space that functions like a vertical urban street. An example of this is Zaha Hadid Architects' Morpheus tower in Macau (2019).

Breaking the Mould: The Leeza SOHO Tower

Located on Lize Road in southwest Beijing, the Leeza SOHO tower anchors the new Fengtai business district – a growing financial and transport hub between the city centre and the recently opened Beijing Daxing International Airport (2019), to the south, also designed by Zaha Hadid Architects. The new business district is integral to Beijing's multimodal urban plan to accommodate growth without overburdening the centre. The tower delivers 172,800 square metres (1.86 million square feet) across 45 ellipsoid storeys. The building rises from a sunken courtyard. Its 5G-powered spaces respond to demand from small and medium-sized businesses for flexible and efficient Grade A office space. Like all the other projects of the building developer SOHO China, the task is to create a buzzing entrepreneurial hub gathering and networking hundreds of small businesses. However, the special challenge here is to create such a business communication hub within a tower – so far the only tall tower trying to deliver the SOHO concept. The solution is provided by the idea of the mega-atrium.

This spiralling, pulsating void is the tallest atrium in the world, and probably one of the brightest. The dramatic verticality and transparency is reminiscent of the tallest Gothic spaces.

Entering these spaces delivers a viscerally uplifting experience, reminiscent of the tallest Gothic cathedrals

The connectivity of the site is exceptional, adjacent to the business district's rail station at the intersection of five new lines currently under construction on Beijing's Subway network. Leeza SOHO's site is diagonally dissected by an underground Subway service tunnel. Straddling this tunnel, the tower's design divides its volume into two halves enclosed by a single facade shell. The emerging space between these two halves extends the full height of the tower, creating the world's tallest atrium at 194.15 metres (637 feet) which rotates through the building as the tower rises to realign the upper floors with Lize Road to the north. This rotation of the mega-atrium intertwines Leeza SOHO's two halves in a dynamic *pas de deux* with connecting sky bridges on levels 13, 24, 35 and 45; the glazed atrium facade gives panoramic views across the city and invites views from the outside in. The twisting surfaces of the atrium give rhythm and dynamism to the space and also facilitate and vary the views up and down the atrium, revealing more than a straight wall would. The sky bridges serve as structural ties and punctuate the free flow of the space.

Leeza SOHO's atrium acts as a public square for the new business district, visually linking all spaces within the tower and creating a new civic space for Beijing that is directly connected to the city's transport network. The atrium brings natural light deep into the building, and also acts as a thermal chimney with an integrated ventilation system that maintains positive pressure at low levels to limit air ingress and provides an effective clean air filtration process within the tower's internal environment.

A Visceral Impact

As with both the Macau and the Leeza Beijing projects, it is important that the mega-atrium is not a hermetic space but also visually connects with the surrounding urban fabric. This reduces vertigo and enhances the sensation of freedom. Entering these spaces delivers a viscerally uplifting experience, reminiscent of the tallest Gothic cathedrals. This too is in architecture's power: delivering a stimulating affective charge that heightens our state of alertness and sense of curiosity, ie the architecture catalyses a state of mind that increases our receptiveness for new knowledge and allows for the intensification of our communicative interactions. ⌂

top: The view from the neighbouring urban spaces and towers into the communication void is as important as the views across the void and the views from inside out. The void draws its audiences in and up the tower.

left: The ellipsoid volume is cladded by full-storey-high shifting shingles that flatten out as the facade approaches the mega-window. This sophisticated parametric variation enhances the plasticity of the volume and, despite the use of only flat panes, gives a very smooth, elegant expression.

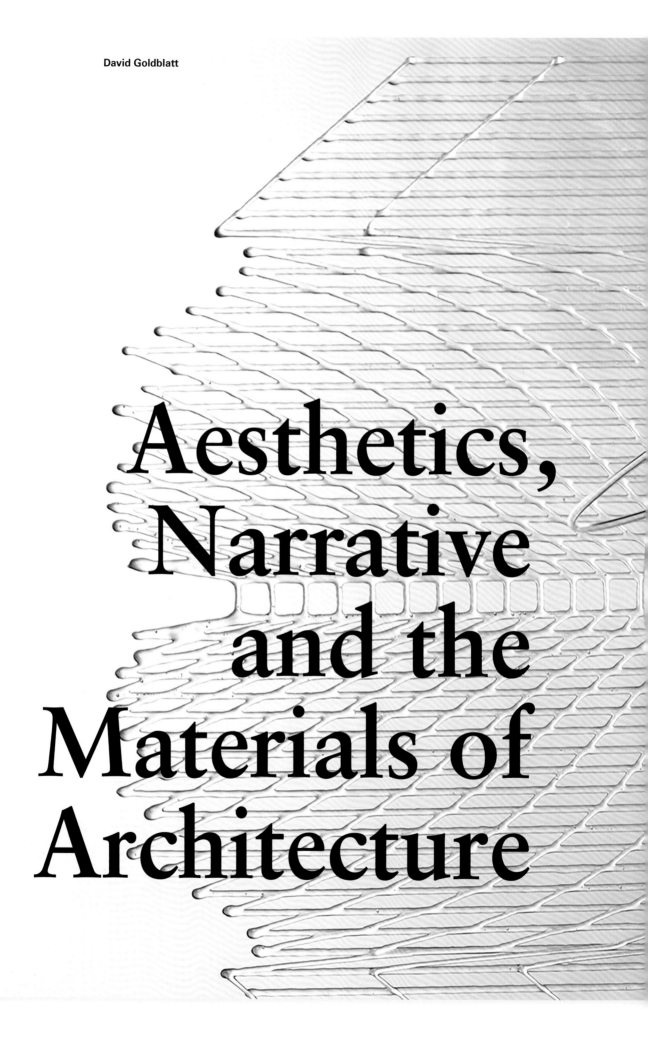

David Goldblatt

Aesthetics, Narrative and the Materials of Architecture

Laia Mogas-Soldevila, Jorge Duro-Royo,
Daniel Lizardo and Neri Oxman,
Water-Based Digital Fabrication,
Media Lab, Massachusetts Institute
of Technology (MIT),
Cambridge, Massachusetts,
2015

Water-Based Digital Fabrication unfolds a novel use in a
narrative based on robotic depositing and biodegradable
material such as bioplastics, extracted from shrimp shells.

All buildings have an impact on us, whether seeing and navigating through and around them for the first time or frequently. Their materiality interacts with us and the streetscape, contributing to our internal and external, sometimes received narrative. **David Goldblatt**, Emeritus Professor of Philosophy at Denison University in Ohio, explains this complex interrelationship and contemplates the effect new materiality might have on this symbiosis.

(P)aper lasts quite as well as paint … later, no one will see the picture, they will see the legend of the picture, the legend that the picture has created … a picture lives by its legend, not by anything else.

— Pablo Picasso quoted by Gertrude Stein in *Picasso*, 1938[1]

There are many ways we become engaged with architecture. Aesthetic experience usually includes the perception of qualities generating feeling or emotion. Our response to artworks is sometimes understood as a tasteful recognition of so-called aesthetic properties such as graceful or elegant. However, as an account of our aesthetic experience of artworks, that kind of response is seriously incomplete – especially when it comes to architecture. Through its complexities and complications, and its position as a negotiable and interactive art, architecture affords sensual encounters that are neither purely visceral nor grasped all at once.

Interwoven in these brief remarks is an attempt to show that our experience of architecture is often, in part, a reaction to the materials of its construction. We might see, then, that a pure aesthetic attitude towards architecture is more myth than reality and that the hegemony of form can, on occasion, be overturned as its material takes prominence.

A key question here is: How does architecture make an impact? One way to answer this question is to say that some architecture affords a cultural impact to the degree that it is part of a meaning-making narrative – where narrative is defined as a story that connects a succession of episodes or events, objects or associations, metaphorical or historical, so that taken together it makes sense.

It should be obvious that we do not come to architecture as *tabulae rasae* and that buildings do not exist isolated from their history and the culture in which they are embedded. Buildings sometimes carry with them their own narratives – their places in site-specific histories and their stories of more cultural or cosmic relevance. The *materials* out of which buildings are formed are often causal factors provoking our aesthetic response. Let us begin with the philosopher Martin Heidegger's insights on the essentiality of the materiality of artworks.

Art and Materiality
In his classic essay 'The Origin of the Work of Art' (1950) Heidegger introduces his careful inquiry by stressing the importance of the material out of which art entities are made. In what he calls 'the thingly aspect of the work of art', Heidegger makes a point about the ontology of artworks *and* our experience of them. He says, 'We … have to take artworks as they are encountered by those who experience and enjoy them. But even the much-vaunted aesthetic experience cannot get around the thingly aspect of the artwork.'[2]

Heidegger understands this thingly aspect as the materials out of which art is made. He writes, 'There is something stony in a work of architecture, wooden in a carving, colored in a painting, spoken in a linguistic work, sonorous in a musical composition.'[3] This material aspect of artworks, he argues, is compelling and outstanding – it is essential in our experience of artworks: 'The thingly element is so irremovably present in the art work that we are compelled rather to say conversely that the architectural work is in stone, the carving is in wood, the painting in color, the linguistic work in speech, the musical composition in sound.'[4]

In Vincent van Gogh's painting *A Pair of Shoes* (1886), 'its leather soles and uppers, joined together by threads and nails', Heidegger imagines the opening up of a clearing, the unconcealedness of the world of the 'woman' who has worn them, and posits an embellishing narrative gleaned in part from the worn-out material inside the pictured shoes, noting 'her slow tread through the far-spreading and ever-uniform furrows of the field swept by a raw wind.'[5] And there is much more to Heidegger's interpretive account, including the loneliness of the field path and the dampness of the earth attached to the shoe's leather.

While the Van Gogh painting is, of course, made of the material of paint, Heidegger is addressing the painting as if he were present to its subject itself as thing, as being in the presence of those peasant shoes, rather than as painted shoes. It is in that face-to-face position that he tells his tale of the shoes, their history, so to speak, and extrapolates a narrative from the shoes' materials – their

Vincent van Gogh,
A Pair of Shoes,
Van Gogh Museum, Amsterdam,
The Netherlands,
1886

Noting the materials out of which these shoes are constructed, the philosopher Martin Heidegger notes their 'thingly' character and narrates an account of the 'woman' who he imagines has worn them in the 'ever-uniform furrows of the field swept by a raw wind' ('The Origin of the Work of Art', in *Poetry, Language, Thought,* trans Albert Hofstadter, Harper Torchbooks (New York), 1971, p 19).

worn leather soles and uppers, their thread and nails. Van Gogh's painting, already unclear as to whether real shoes have been represented, is fictionalised by Heidegger's account.

So it is that in a reflection not privy to the peasant woman herself, the shoes, depicted as 'reliable' objects, conjure up a narrative gleaned from their materiality. The generation of narratives, then, is one way the thingly character of the shoes prompted a response by Heidegger. So too, architecture's thingly character is often what prompts theoretical analysis, which is included in our perceptual account of buildings.

In his *The Truth in Painting* (1987)[6] the philosopher Jacques Derrida takes on art historian Meyer Schapiro's critique of Heidegger's narrative regarding the *ownership* of the pair of depicted shoes. Schapiro's claim, that the shoes belonged to Heidegger, a city dweller, and not to a peasant or a woman, challenges assumptions that lie at the centre of Heidegger's disclosure of truth in Van Gogh's painting. Derrida questions the truth of Schapiro's claim and asks, satirically, why should the shoes be attached to anyone at all? Why a peasant or a city dweller? Why must they even be a pair of shoes? And so, the narrative occasioned by this and other of Van Gogh's shoe paintings has been extended.

Narrative and Architecture

Derrida reminds us of the historical narratives and cultural impacts, the absorption and deep permeation architecture embraces as he argues that the concept of architecture is itself architectural. He says:

Down even to its archaic foundation, the most fundamental concept of architecture has been constructed. This architecture of architecture has a history, it is historical through and through. Its heritage inaugurates the intimacy of our economy, the law of our hearth (*oikos*), our familial, religious and political 'oikonomy,' all the places of birth and death, temple, school, stadium, agora, square, sepulcher.[7]

Derrida's 'architecture of architecture' stands in opposition to the expression 'architecture for architecture's sake' since that manifesto calls for an isolated concept of architecture, independent of its becoming. Whereas Derrida's brand of contextualism sees architecture as it should be: its heritage filtering through nearly all aspects of our lives, a central factor in our architectural experience. Architectural meaning, embedded in the very material of its structure, can be metaphorical or analogical as well as literal as it is captured by its story.

The novelist Mary McCarthy, in her *The Stones of Florence* (1959), connects historical and economic impact with materialisation: 'History, for Florence, is neither a legend nor eternity, and it's a massive weight of rough building stone demanding continual repairs, pressing on the modern city like a debt, blocking progress.'[8] Here, centuries-old stone absorbs the economic story of a modern city. Some of the marble facades of Italian cities, she says, have left tourists with the feeling that the abundance of stone was 'cold and unwelcoming'.[9]

We get a sense of the intermingling of material, history and identity as McCarthy describes the materials of Florence: 'black, grey, dun and bronze are the colours of Florence – the colours of stone and metal, the primitive elements of Nature out of which the first civilizations were hammered – the Stone Age, the Bronze Age, the Iron Age.'[10] And here she reminds us that entire historical periods were named for their materials.

The prevalence of stone throughout the history of architecture dominated aesthetic experience whenever it was used – city walls, castles, banks, estates, ruins. Although hard to articulate, stone provided auditors with feelings of impenetrability, security and durability, even permanence, which was emanated in their presence. While the great cathedrals of Europe imposed diminution by virtue of their powerful scale, stone countered that by offering historical endurance.

Barbed Wire

Impact comes in many ways. Take a different building material – barbed wire. The impact of barbed wire on the American West from the 1860s onwards ended the open range that existed from the Rio Grande to the Canadian plains and changed the cattle industry forever. 'Barbed wire has always been regarded as the thing that stripped the range of that quality so dear to the hearts of old-timers – freedom.'[11] Think here of the Cole Porter tune

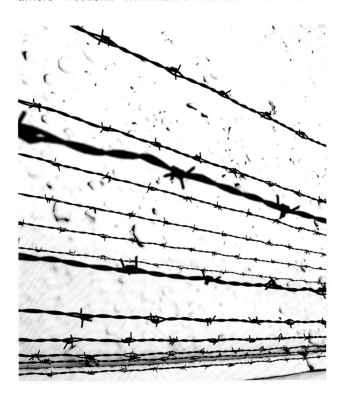

Petr Kratochvila,
Barbed Wire,
2012

Barbed wire helped to end the open range of the American West from the 1860s onwards and became part of an evolving narrative that included First World War trench warfare, concentration camps and prison walls. It is a good example of how one perceptual mode of material provokes another and how narratives of materials can change over time.

'Don't Fence Me In' (1934) as a later personal response to an American free range out where the west commences.

However, barbed wire's history continues to be sinister and it carries with it evolving narratives – trench warfare, concentration camps and prison walls, with an aesthetic spectrum that includes repulsion and estrangement. Barbed wire is a good example of how certain historical events can replace current aesthetic impacts with new ones. And barbed wire is an example of how one mode of perception, the visual, effectively translates into another, the tactile; as we are inclined to imagine what it would be like to get caught up in its iron thorns.

To help understand the difference of degree of aesthetic response among materials, we might think of another form of fencing: the chain link fence utilised by Frank Gehry (at his residence in Santa Monica, California, 1978) and Robert Venturi (at the Guild House, Philadelphia, 1963). While each generates a feeling of being unwelcome, the effect is less intimidating than barbed wire – as if the aesthetic response was measured by juxtaposition. In this context we might think of iron bars commonly used on the windows of low-storey apartments but also in the transformation of the old Hong Kong prison into the Tai Kwun cultural hub (2017) where doors to former jail cells were left in place – black bars contrasting with white walls. The impact of the Tai Kwun centre is partially determined by having its story tied to a female prison: leaving the cell doors intact is an obvious reminder of its history – the materialisation of memory.

If we think of the ubiquitous use of glass curtain walls in late modernism, we might recognise the cool silence, a distance built between person and corporation, observer and building, an alienating projection to accompany, in something of a paradox, its transparency. Philip Johnson, famous for his home, his Glass House in New Canaan, Connecticut (1949), was also the architect of the Crystal Cathedral, near Los Angeles (1980). The Cathedral, with its enormous glass facade, is a good example of how a site for religion can be cold and off-putting, despite its purpose.

Glass, for all its reflectivity and invisibility, is a material that does not age well. But it was, I think, a certain indifference that glass has to any local narrative that made modernism an easy target for Robert Venturi, Denise Scott Brown and Steven Izenour's seminal critique *Learning from Las Vegas* (1972) by calling attention to the warming of neon and friendly signage appealing to the fun of tourism, that occasioned the inviting decorated sheds of Vegas.[12] Las Vegas has changed since that time, however, and what Venturi *et al* called 'the duck' has taken on other architectural references, like the Egyptian pyramids and the canals of Venice.

Bringing a vernacular trait into elite construction is Foster + Partners and Heatherwick Studio's Bund Finance Centre in Shanghai (2017), where vertically hung bronze rods are detailed into bamboo imitations and placed in diagonal layers across a facade that has a surprisingly

Heatherwick Studio and Foster + Partners,
Fosun Foundation,
Bund Finance Centre,
Shanghai, China,
2017

top: Visitors can view the bamboo-like tassels on the terrace where vernacular details enter an elite architecture by referencing elements of the Asian natural environment and the materials of scaffolding.

above: Embossed foil test: close-up detail of texture on a tassel mock-up.

musical affect on a perceiver. The notched and node-like bamboo embraces a natural history of Asia, but also an artefact of building as it is a key material used for scaffolding, bringing the vernacular to express the process as well as the product of its construction and so constituting in part a narrative response to this Finance Centre.

Architecture is itself an ingredient of broad and deep narratives. We saw this in what Derrida had to say about its wide historical contexts. Perhaps more than other arts, instances of architecture are part of the story of the warming of the planet – its endangerment by floods and fire but also its notorious contributions to it. Certain of the production of its materials, such as cement, have played a role in causing serious environmental damage that if not minimised can produce hazardous emissions of greenhouse gases.

On the other hand, energy-efficient buildings can utilise materials that approach renewable self-sustaining capabilities. For example, Jeanne Gang's Solar Carve Tower (2019) juxtaposing New York City's High Line. The High Line is a story of the conversion of a dead elevated freight railroad into a green-space park encouraging pedestrian traffic. Studio Gang has joined that story as well as the story of a troubled planet. The massing and sculpted shape of the 10-storey commercial building is designed to maximise the sunlight and fresh air that reach the High Line by 'carving' into the tower according to the incident angle of the sun's path. Increasing its environmental credentials are the different types of low-emissivity, insulated glass for the facade, whose formulations are tuned to function and solar position. Much of the glass is low-reflexivity, reducing glare below and helping to prevent fatal collisions by birds. Innovative materials can form the basis of environmental responsibility by promoting sustainable design practices that can reduce waste and lessen the demand for quantities of material.

Studio Gang, Solar Carve Tower,
New York, New York,
2019

Solar Carve explores how shaping architecture in response to solar access and other site-specific criteria can have a positive impact on its environment while utilising various forms of glass.

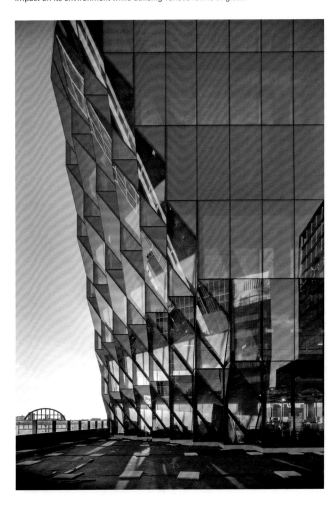

The glazing system has been geometrically optimised into a pattern of three-dimensional facets that articulate the carved sections of the tower.

Future Materials and Aesthetic Response

Humphrey Lyttelton, the English hornman, was asked where he thought jazz was going. His reply was: 'If I knew where jazz was going, I'd be there already.'[13] While we don't know exactly where architecture is going, there are sets of still-experimental materials, yet unapplied to actual construction, which may give us some indication. We can imagine, for example, a material of silky feel and look, but with the strength to sustain a structural function, presenting itself as a satisfying yet unfamiliar experience.

Digital technology, through images and 3D models, makes it easier to imagine futuristic materials come alive in their use without the complexity that accompanies built architecture. Out of labs come a startling array of colour and pattern, texture and fluidity, accompanied in part by the shock of the new. Architects will have options to control design with materials from point zero aimed at new modes of building. Out of the Massachusetts Institute of Technology (MIT) labs, for example, come water-based materials that not only can fold in new and unexpected ways, but are also biodegradable, sustainable, and so enter narratives that are ecologically viable as well as aesthetically original. We can think of evolving forms as a kind of proto-architecture, coming quickly and with confidence on the way towards construction.

Laia Mogas-Soldevila, Jorge Duro-Royo, Daniel Lizardo and Neri Oxman, Water-Based Digital Fabrication, Media Lab, Massachusetts Institute of Technology (MIT), Cambridge, Massachusetts, 2015

The degrees of opacity in these water-based fabrications combine for a narrative that is ecologically friendly with distribution patterns that generate self-folding behaviour and gradients of opacity and mechanical performance.

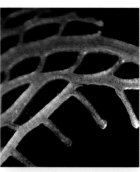

The geometrically graded
bending capacity of
the biopolymer matrix
and cellulose fibre filler
combines a potential
aesthetic response to
pattern with surprising
structural strength.

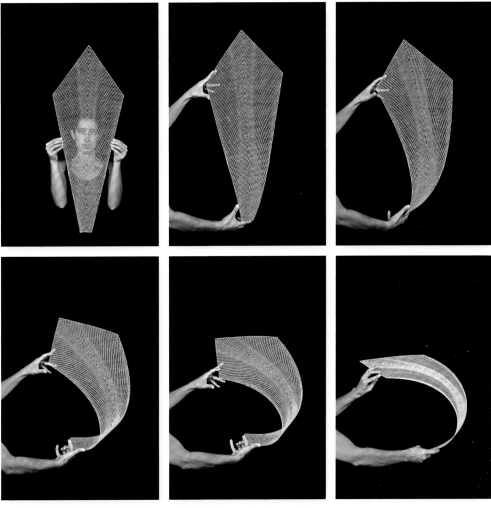

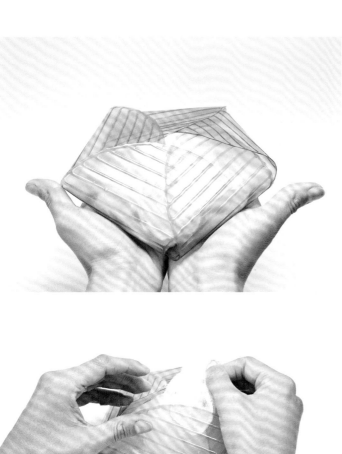

Created with the Water-Based Digital Fabrication platform, bioplastic-based fully recyclable packaging products hold the promise of a surprising new aesthetic for their patterns, textures, and potential for prompting new narratives.

Final Remarks

Distinct from other art forms, with architecture we move in and around buildings, for the first time or time after time and, as such, we ourselves are elements in an architectural story. We know that dramatic episodes take place inside architecture, later to become told and retold. But buildings, too, show themselves as ingredients of tellings. Their materials can provoke age and strength, clarity and reflection, grace and beauty, political power and corporate wealth. There are other ways of embedding meaning in architecture, but narrative is one mode of rendering meaning – one way architecture can mark its cultural impact and the way we understand ourselves, which may well be what art is all about.[14] ⅅ

Notes

1. Gertrude Stein, *Picasso*, Beacon Press (New York), 1938, p 27.
2. Martin Heidegger, 'The Origin of the Work of Art', in *Poetry, Language, Thought,* trans Albert Hofstadter, Harper Torchbooks (New York), 1971, p 19.
3. *Ibid.*
4. *Ibid* p 19
5. *Ibid* p 20.
6. Jacques Derrida, *The Truth in Painting*, trans Geoff Bennington and Ian McLeod, University of Chicago Press (Chicago), 1987, pp 259–382.
7. Jacques Derrida, 'Jacques Derrida in Discussion with Christopher Norris', *AA Files 12* (1986), pp 65–75.
8. Mary McCarthy, *The Stones of Florence*, Harvest / Harcourt, Brace & World (New York), 1959, p 23.
9. *Ibid* p 21.
10. *Ibid* p 35.
11. Mark H Brown and WR Felton, *Before Barbed Wire*, Bramhall House (New York), 1956, p 9.
12. Robert Venturi, Denise Scott Brown and Steven Izenour, *Learning from Las Vegas*, The MIT Press (Cambridge, MA), 1977, pp 90–92.
13. Quoted in Peter Winch, *The Idea of a Social Science*, Routledge & Kegan Paul (London), 1958, pp 93–4.
14. Many thanks for their help: Alissa Anderson of Studio Gang, Leon Yi-Liang Ko of Contemporary Architecture Practice and Laia Mogas Soldevila of Tufts University.

SHANG
BUND

HAI
THE IMPACT OF CONTEXT

Designer **Thomas Heatherwick** has an international reputation honed by a series of buildings that have audacious formal articulations. These buildings often exhibit the repetition of architectural elements, yet the same base element is used in an almost infinite array of combinations. Here he describes the thoughts, concepts, materiality and surface treatments of his Fosun Foundation building for the Bund Finance Centre in Shanghai.

Heatherwick Studio and Foster + Partners, Fosun Foundation, Bund Finance Centre, Shanghai, China, 2017

Close-up detail of the Fosun Foundation kinetic facade. The three layers of moving veils can create a diverse range of visual effects and openness, thus allowing the space to be used for a variety of events.

The Bund in the great port city of Shanghai, China, refers to a mile-long embankment of the Huangpu River. The architecturally eclectic buildings in this commercial area, in what was once the Shanghai International Settlement, date to several eras of colonial and postcolonial mercantile activity. They reflect a variety of influences, in particular American and British. Among the earlier structures are the America Club, built in the 1920s in American Georgian style, and the Customs House of that same period, with its imitation Big Ben tower and clock. The bustling area now is deeply identified with the thriving Chinese economy and Shanghai's important place as one of China's most dynamic modern cities and a centre for international banking and commerce.

My studio won a competition to develop a masterplan along the Bund at a significant juncture between the old and new parts of the district and across the river from Pudong. Developed jointly with Foster + Partners, it was the last undeveloped site and was surrounded by the colonial buildings, Shanghai's old town, and the new skyscrapers in the financial district. The 420,000-square-metre (4.5-million-square-foot) development called for eight buildings, including a hotel, office and retail space, among them a pair of towers, plus an arts centre to act as a focal point for the district. The buildings define the 'end point' to Shanghai's most famous thoroughfare, Zhongshan Road.

Heatherwick Studio and Foster + Partners, Bund Finance Centre, Shanghai, China, 2017

A palette of crafted stone and bronze details gives the buildings a jewel-like quality. Helping to create an extra layer of dimension, the detailing draws inspiration from historical buildings along the Bund.

Heatherwick Studio and Foster + Partners, Bund Finance Centre, Shanghai, China, 2017

Aerial view of the Bund Finance Cent... along the Shanghai waterfront. The new development was conceived as a point of connection between the ol... town and the new financial district.

Our approach was to consider how elements of the masterplan could be designed in relation to the precinct's site neighbours, rather than appearing as overscaled elements without a connection to the context. Another major challenge was to create a new public space that would connect the old town and new financial district. The building scales were deliberately staggered to locate the two taller buildings of 180 metres (590 feet) close to the skyscrapers in the newer district, and smaller buildings towards the historic part of the city. The smaller buildings surround a new public piazza and create a social focus at the heart of the district.

Organised like slim, extruded volumes, all of the buildings have intricate detailing at their base that pares back as they rise to give a sense of lightness towards the top. At lower levels, the finishes include textured granite cladding and bronze detailing that creates interest up close; from afar the granite, glass and bronze form a consistent material palette across the site. To relate to the heritage of the Bund buildings and to give visual and textural richness, we wanted to avoid the effect of a simple, flat rainscreen. Working with a local factory we tested a lot of different materials and finishes and eventually devised a bespoke cladding system that would add a distinct sense of place and that also felt connected with the older parts of the city. The materials needed to combine the latest environmental technology with traditional methods of making. Marked by a continuous surface pattern, the stone sheets combine mechanised production and hand finishing to give a rippled effect while also being robust enough to endure the extremes of temperature in the region.

Heatherwick Studio and Foster + Partners, Fosun Foundation, Bund Finance Centre, Shanghai, China, 2017

View of the completed Fosun Foundation at street level. The arts centre acts as a focal point for the district.

Our focus for the Bund project was to try to invent a new type of place that responded to the history of the city and the layers of cultural influence that have made it so special

eatherwick Studio and Foster +
Partners, Fosun Foundation, Bund
inance Centre, Shanghai, China,
2017

errace inside the Fosun Foundation, behind the
inetic facade where visitors can view the tassels
p close.

A New Type of Place

The retail and cultural buildings are framed in the hand-carved stone and use a high-performance glazing system that helps to passively regulate temperature and solar gain. The specially crafted stone with rich bronze details gives a jewel-like aesthetic to the buildings, helping to create a language of materiality that draws on Chinese historical references to the bronze finishes found in the much earlier buildings along the Bund. As many cities around the world are becoming more and more like each other, there is a danger of eventually having no unique cities any more. Our focus for the Bund project was to try to invent a new type of place that responded to the history of the city and the layers of cultural influence that have made it so special.

The two landmark towers in the south of the site step down towards each other in a reinterpretation of the traditional gateway arch. More heavily detailed at their base, they become less detailed higher up, giving them a feeling of lightness and elegance. Careful consideration was given to the texture of the buildings at ground level and the experience for pedestrians: the facade is based on a sequence of extruding volumes that are pulled out from the lower floors and unify the entire scheme to create a sense of place. Whether we are designing a London bus that will be used for people to travel to work every day of the week or a building that thousands of people will work in or pass by, we always approach each design from a human perspective and scale. Buildings can be vast but they can still be soulful and rooted in their context.

At the core of the public piazza is the 4,000-square-metre (43,000-square-foot) Fosun Foundation – a multilayer, cantilevered venue that acts as a symbolic focal point. It serves as an event space, performance venue and arts gallery. We designed this to be the heart of the development, overlooking and forming a physical and empathetic connection with the public piazza. The theatre building is designed as a place for spectacle. Intensive research into theatres of all kinds, but especially the local traditions, led to the idea for a moving facade, something both meaningful with its reference to theatrical effects and that would draw visitors towards the building while also bringing an identity to the district. The building design aims to have an emotional resonance for visitors as well as being flexible and interesting for artists and curators.

Like the tradition of open stages in Chinese theatre, the facade, wrapped by moving 'veils' of metal tubes, can adapt the space to create a diverse range of visual effects and opacities. The space itself is designed to be flexible. The immediate inspiration for the moving facade's mechanism came from an automobile production plant, where the car chassis are suspended from a giant track. Local engineers from Tongji University helped with the logistics of the three-track system that can move three veils of tubular metal tassels. A total of 675 individual magnesium alloy tassels vary from 2 to 16 metres (6 to 52 feet) long.

Heatherwick Studio
and Foster + Partners,
Fosun Foundation,
Bund Finance Centre,
Shanghai, China,
2017

Scale prototype of the kinetic
facade to test the mechanism's
tolerance against wind loads.
The prototype was built with
146 tassels, with each layer of
tassels and set of motors tested
to ensure that the final facade
could resist upwards of Level
12 typhoon winds.

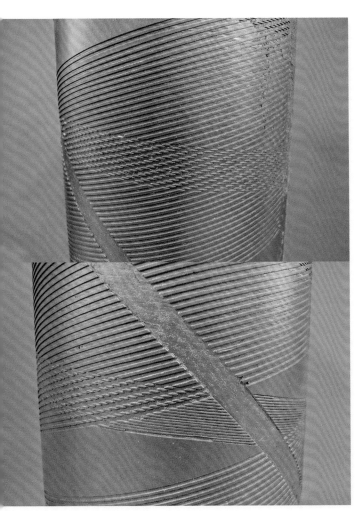

They are embossed with a pattern inspired by ropes, knots and Chinese weaving, each terminating with a vitreous-enamelled steel cap in three variations of red. Each layer of tassels is coated with titanium nitride to give a subtly different shade of bronze.

While the mechanism that moves the veils of tassels is relatively simple, an exhaustive effort went into testing the materials and mechanical performance in order to make a moving facade on this scale. For example, the moving veils had to withstand a Level 12 typhoon wind without the tassels touching each other. Achieving this degree of robustness involved building a prototype with 146 tassels to test the effect of wind loads on them. We were restricted to two tonnes per linear metre for the tassels, track and motor. There are six motors in total which includes three backups. The effect of the movement of the overlapping tassel layers past one another in opposite directions is profound and hypnotic. The building facade can almost entirely open up to create views out onto the Bund and reveal the stage to the public, making a performance space that is connected to the public realm, or it can be a more formal, closed and intimate interior space – or somewhere in between these states depending on what is required.

Conscious that Shanghai today is one of China's most dynamic modern cities, from the start of the project the studio decided to utilise the amazing craft-making skills that are available in China but not elsewhere. Our objective was to create a district with an extra dimension through craft and detail. ⧉

Close-up details of embossing tests on a tassel mockup. The patterns were inspired by ropes, knots and Chinese weaving.

Inspection of the first full tassel produced. Each layer of tassels was coated with titanium nitride to give a subtly different shade of bronze.

Ali Rahim and Hina Jamelle

Disjunctive Continuity and the

Contemporary Architecture Practice,
NJCTTQ Headquarters,
Nanjing, China,
2019

The sculptural stair was conceived of
as a form, inserted into the space and
further reinforced through the flush
light that cradles the form.

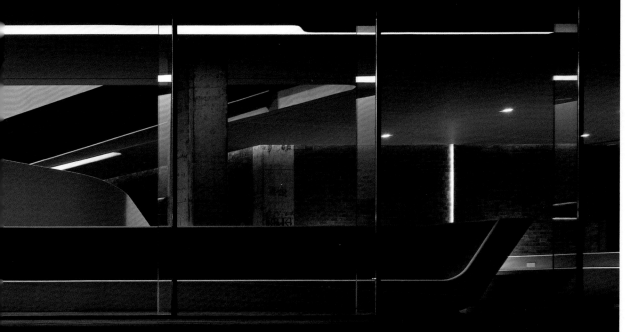

Aesthetics of the Seam

Guest-Editors **Ali Rahim and Hina Jamelle** teach graduate Architecture at the University of Pennsylvania Weitzman School of Design and are the co-founders of Contemporary Architectural Practice (CAP) based in New York and Shanghai. Here they lead us through a brief history of the pros and cons of the architectural digital project of the last 25 years, advocating a return to detailing and the careful juxtaposition of materials, collaboratively working with numerous manufacturers and contractors to create architectures of nested, multiscaled and multivalent seams.

Since the 1990s, the digital project in architecture has been about the diminishment of the detail – that non-spectacular, devilish aspect of putting together a building. It has tended to privilege the uninterrupted smooth and seamless form, a pivot from both the extroverted disjointedness of Postmodernism and the logical yet deceptive pragmatism of Modernism.

While Modernist theory called for clarity in architectural assembly, its practical manifestations proved otherwise.[1] The Miesian mantra regarding honest expression of material structure was often uttered in vain. In neither Mies's classic Barcelona Pavilion (1929) nor his New York Seagram Building (1962) is there a clear expression of construction. The Barcelona Pavilion's steel structure and partitions were veneered with onyx and marble to make it appear monolithic. The Seagram Building's original steel columns and beams were caked in code-required concrete for fireproofing. Displeased with that particular form of structural expression, Mies revised the detail to include a steel profile covering the concrete-clad columns, replicated across the building's entire enclosure to give the impression of a uniform facade.[3] In the hands of an architect like Mies van der Rohe, the disjunctions between the conceptual goals of Modernism, the aesthetic goals of its designers, and the ambivalence of the detail could be veiled with great success.[4]

Contemporary Architecture Practice,
Reebok flagship store,
Shanghai, China,
2004

Though the store interior is composed of a distinct form, the primary aesthetic goal is achieved through the vectors that move across it to produce an intricate and detailed assembly.

While Postmodern architects launched a poignant critique of the false unities of Modernism, they also inherited and replicated the same approach to details used by their predecessors. Whether or not that critique created good spaces or aesthetics is a debate long past its due date; however, the potential of disjunction as a creative principle is worth re-examination in the new technological landscape.

In the digital era, architects left behind the question of material expression, assembly and the detail all together. The age of the computer was the age of form, smoothness and a material-less architecture with little basis in material reality. Simultaneously, the computer model and the building image became more important than the building itself. It was assumed that the wall cavities of digital projects would be filled with the structural and mechanical necessities required to make them work. Architects set aside the question of building assembly in favour of the question of inception and the digital design process. For the last three decades, the most talked-about feature of architecture has not been its buildings, but rather its process-driven design. In this digital culture, the image became the project.

Intricacy and Materiality

Developments in computer technology and software since the 1990s have given designers unrivalled capacities to create aesthetic effects over the early generation of digital architects and their predecessors. The new aesthetic frontier circumvents building form and focuses on the design of the detail to produce highly intricate and varied assemblies composed of advanced materials. Rather than reproducing the aesthetic of the computer interface, architects can now engage the material world with all the tools that have been developed during the digital age. This engagement, including a strict attention to detail, is an axiom of the work of Contemporary Architecture Practice. The goal of this disjunctive continuity is to achieve familiar plurality within unity or, if you will, diversity in a singular, overall expression. Disjunctive continuity frees us to move from detail to form, rather than the other way around. It is an attempt to bring practice and theory together, a target missed by both the Modernists and the early digital technologists.

Contemporary Architecture Practice has always been interested in the role of the detail in the production of an aesthetic goal. Some of the firm's most widely known projects demonstrate its obsession with intricacy, assembly and materiality. The Reebok flagship store in Shanghai (2004) is an early example of the practice's desire to develop intricacy in its work. The project features a prominent bifurcating tubular form suspended within the shell of an existing building. This form is neither smooth nor seamless; instead, a field of vectors wraps the surface, splitting it with stairs, shelving and slots for lighting. The construction and assembly method are not expressed true to form; rather, the joinery and seaming are designed for aesthetic effect. The seams move in the opposite direction of the assembly joints to conceal them, a technique that is utilised in much of the practice's work.

IWI Orthodontics in Tokyo (2011) picked up where Reebok left off to develop a new approach to materiality. Rather than beginning the project with a form and

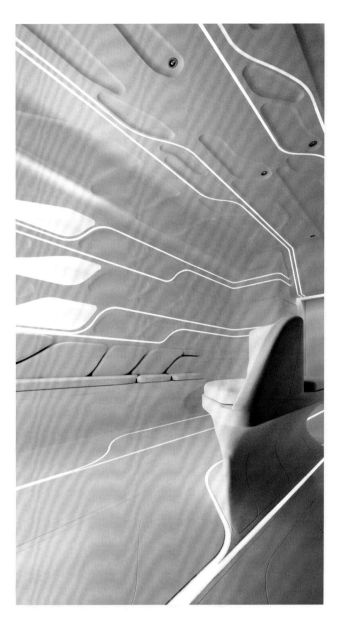

Contemporary Architecture Practice,
IWI Orthodontics,
Tokyo, Japan,
2011

The IWI Orthodontics interior is composed of many different materials: CNC-milled calcium silicate, gypsum board, micro suede, acrylic and more. All these materials are detailed and connected through a field of vectors to achieve a cohesive aesthetic for the project.

articulating it, the space was conceived as a series of vectors wrapping the floor, walls and ceiling that define detailed material connections. The ceilings are milled calcium-silicate panels that wrap the walls and meet more durable milled engineered wood panels. The seams are integrated with the furniture, which has the same form as the wall panels but is made of soft foam wrapped in micro-suede. If Reebok demonstrates intricacy, IWI demonstrates variegated materials achieving a cohesive aesthetic. Both projects are consistent in their respective aesthetics and attempt to integrate architectural performance – HVAC, lighting, waterproofing, fireproofing and even seismic features – into singular detailed assemblies.

Disjunctive Continuity

These investigations have continued in the recently completed project for the Nanjing Chia Tai-Tianqing Pharmaceutical Company (NJCTTQ) in Nanjing, China (2019). The intention here was to move the practice's design work from the intricate and highly articulated legacy of its previous designs, including Reebok and IWI, to a sophisticated incorporation of multi-material richness and varied aesthetics within the same project. This led to the concept of 'disjunctive continuity' – where the construction of a building may be the same throughout, but the aesthetic goals, details and material assemblies can shift as needed to suit the architect's intent. This was achieved while producing a restrained aesthetic for a high-tech company looking to brand itself through the finely tuned opulence of its new company headquarters.

The design for the new NJCTTQ headquarters and factory complex sprawls over six buildings and 140,000 square metres (1.5 million square feet) for functions as diverse as an educational centre with auditorium, research and design facilities, laboratories, corporate offices, meeting spaces including VIP and board rooms, a research and development centre, and a cafeteria that feeds a thousand employees a day. Contemporary Architecture Practice conceived a series of details that developed into various forms within the existing envelope that are disjunct from one another. These forms are connected through various independent devices such as floor seams and ceiling patterns.

Disjunctive continuity is developed at several scales in the NJCTTQ project, including those of the detail, material and form. Different methods were used to achieve the practice's goals, including the development of details that conceal or reveal edges and joints. Details are crucial as they control the aesthetics of the material assembly and form. Seams accentuate or diminish the assembly. Materials nest into and layer on top of one another. Details are developed into objects, and these objects are inserted into specific spaces. The exact techniques of assembly vary, but the goal is the same: to achieve a visually cohesive aesthetic composed of details that are both different and disjunct. For the NJCTTQ project, this was achieved in a number of ways.

Gallery construction. Precast glass-reinforced concrete panels are assembled with transverse joints. The major seams and accents run cross-directionally to subvert the reading of the construction logic.

Contemporary Architecture Practice,
Nanjing Chia Tai-Tianqing
Pharmaceutical Company
(NJCTTQ) headquarters,
Nanjing, China,
2019

The reception desk has the same material palette as the meeting booth, but is configured differently. The details of the reception desk emphasise the aesthetic theme of the project: materials nested into one another, revealed through precise detailing. The overall mass of the desk is set in contrast with the lightness of the engineered wood panelling and enhanced through a concealed LED around its edge.

First, seams move across material assemblies instead of delineating them. The interview booth uses four disjunct materials at different scales. White Corian is nested into a frame of engineered wood. A grey composite is layered over this surface with an LED edge that makes it appear to float. The booth is nested into a cove in the gypsum board ceiling. The cove's interior is wrapped with engineered wood that connects to the engineered composite of the booth frame, but also acts to conceal the lighting and mechanical systems. The composite material reappears on the interior of the booth as a sound absorption material. The continuity of the booth is achieved through seaming details. The seam is indifferent to changes in materiality and moves from the gypsum board ceiling, wraps around the engineered wood and grey composite of the booth walls, and continues to the carpet covering the floor.

Seams are also used to separate the same material in different ways. Four walls delineate the gallery, each of which has a nested backlit display box and acts as a gallery display space. The ceiling and floor details produce a floating effect,

giving the space a light and soft yet tailored quality. There are clear moments of continuity through the curvilinear geometry, but also moments of discontinuity where the walls disrupt the flow paths and create moments for display and observation. The details of the display wall connections to the ceiling are key to the disjunctive quality of the space. The seams of the ceiling move across the seams of the assembled glass-fibre-reinforced panels. The section of the ceiling has two mirrored adjoining fillets separated by a distinct groove that creates a shadowy transition between the wall and the ceiling. This, along with the flush lighting detail, its adjoining seam and a larger concave section of the ceiling reinforce the nested quality of the gallery walls. These details work to emphasise the walls as individual objects inserted into the space and enhance their performance as spaces for viewing.

The seams then scale up to form larger monolithic volumes nested with different materials. The stair that connects the main lobby to the training centre is a large monolithic form prefabricated offsite in one piece and then installed in the space. The handrail is carved into the interior of the form.

The gallery is composed of four disjunctive objects inserted into the space. The seams and flush lights reinforce the object quality of the display walls.

Three seams of varying widths located on the ceiling enhance the form's presence in the space. A fine seam of 5 millimetres highlights the opening of the stair, a wider seam of 20 millimetres masks linear diffusers, and the largest seam of 25 millimetres houses a light fixture that cradles the stair and nearby bench. Wood stairs are inserted in the interior of the monolithic form. There is a reveal designed into the edge of the stair for LED lights. Wooden bookcases are nested within and on the sides of the larger form. The wood profile is not shown on the perimeter of the bookcase in order to emphasise the nested quality of the wood. The stair and bench allow for the nesting of materials in order to enhance the experience of the space's larger volumetric qualities.

Seams also shape the spaces. Cast aluminium inset seams are used in the research and design facility to separate the black-and-white micro-terrazzo flooring. These are mirrored by wide black seams on the ceiling flanked by two finer black seams that contain lighting fixtures and linear diffusers. The floor and ceiling lines delineate the disjunctive office spaces and conference areas around them. The same aluminium floor seams are used to formulate the edge of the material change between hard micro-terrazzo and soft carpeting. As the floor material changes, the ceiling lowers and changes in material from drywall to acoustic panels for open offices. The edges of the acoustic panels are covered with drywall. The micro-terrazzo floor continues and stops at the edge of the conference room, which is made entirely of flush abutting glass panels to enhance its shape and object-like qualities. The ceiling pushes up within the conference room and is highlighted by an LED light detail that runs around the perimeter of the conference room with a wide seam for return air. The floor and ceiling seams shape the elliptical spaces around them and provide a sleekness intended to reflect the progressive nature of the research and development department.

Finally, the repetition of seams multiplies the material intricacy of the space. The auditorium is an accumulation of striated sections. Each is detailed with engineered wood, acoustic panels covered in fabric, and drywall. The drywall is flush with the grey fabric acoustic panels and abuts the wood panels. The scale of the grey panels is broken down by an additional seam moving vertically and parallel to the shape of the panel. The seams continue onto the ceiling where the distance between them is reduced and widened again when they meet the panels on the opposite side of the auditorium. As they move down the wall and meet the floor, the seams continue and separate the hard wood from the carpet. This detail is multiplied seven times and is highlighted by continuous strips of LED lighting. Each striated section is offset by the height of a stair, and each stair offset allows the ceiling to house lighting, ventilation and acoustic components. Repeating the sections seven times creates the overall visual impact of the auditorium being spatially disjunct in longitudinal section yet aesthetically cohesive in material composition.

A New (Re-)Turn

Recognising a new turn, or re-turn, in the digital project, and in moving from the detail to the aesthetics of form, Contemporary Architecture Practice develops designs

above: The glass conference spaces of the research and development centre are used to break up the open office spaces. The sloped detail around these spaces strengthens the reading of the glass conference spaces as forms nested into the ceiling.

right: The sculptural stair connects the training centre to the main lobby and is one of the prominent design elements of the project. Conceived as a form inserted into the project, this is supported through the flush light and the seam in the ceiling that cradle the stair.

bove: The long axis of the auditorium is shaped for acoustic optimisation, he short axis has been broken down through material striation moving ransverse to the direction of the form. The material striation is composed of ands of wood panels, fabric acoustic panels, and gypsum board.

that maximise the diversity of effects within a single project that are intricate, responsive and multilayered yet uncompromising in their overall aesthetics. The practice builds upon Modernist pragmatism towards the relationship between materials and details and directly addresses Modernist incongruities between theory and practice. Its interest is in intensifying the desire for the object by removing indices of its assembled components and establishing deeper, multidimensional relationships between details and materials. Using technology for the design and manufacturing of the practice's work enables the details to be altered from one instance to another within the same project, including changing the sequencing of materials, cradling of materials, and nesting of one material into another. This is only possible by designing in three dimensions and working directly with fabrication facilities to construct adjoining materials with fine tolerances that match its designs exactly. This allows the seams in the designs to highlight and subvert attributes of form. Elements with quantitative and qualitative differences can be brought together in ways that form disjunctive features within a visually continuous and aesthetically cohesive space. Experimenting with disjunctions between materials and assemblies can now be viewed as a new direction for architectural discourse with compelling aesthetic outcomes. ⌂

Notes

1. William Curtis, *Modern Architecture Since 1900*, Phaidon (London), 1996, p 271.
2. Detlef Mertins, *Mies*, Phaidon Press (London and New York), 2014, p 148.
3. Phyllis Lambert, *Building Seagram*, Yale University Press (New Haven, CT), 2013, p 109.
4. Edward R Ford, *The Architectural Detail*, Princeton Architectural Press (New York), 2011, pp 147–9.

Mater
Intrica

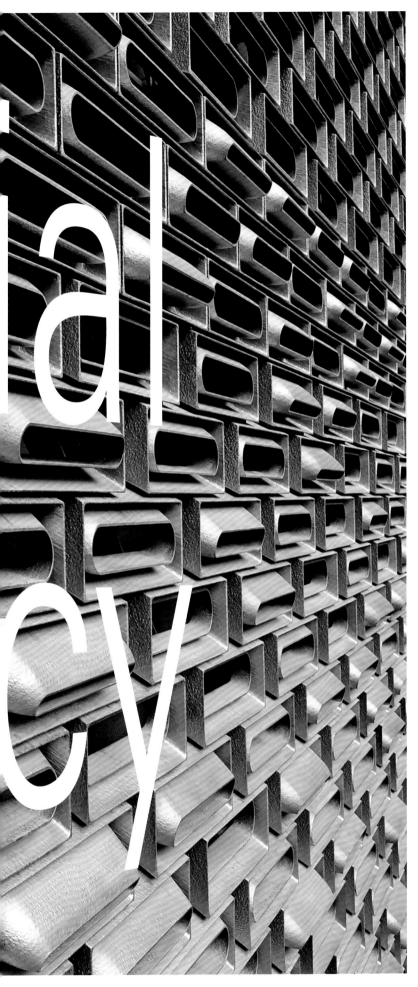

Herzog & de Meuron's Tai Kwun centre for heritage and arts in Hong Kong has an innovative and spectacular facade. It is both a sun- and rain-screen made of rough-cast aluminium units. **Ascan Mergenthaler**, senior partner at the firm, guides us through the design process, the detailing, and particularly how the facade turns corners, the inspiration for its jointing coming from traditional masonry bonding.

Herzog & de Meuron,
Tai Kwun centre for
heritage and arts,
Hong Kong,
2018

Corner detail. The recycled aluminium facade is rough cast, giving the aluminium blocks a distinctive architectural expression and materiality.

Colonial Hong Kong's Central Police Station, the Central Magistracy, and the Victoria Prison, built in the mid-19th century, once had a commanding view of the city and harbour of the former British colony. By the time the site was decommissioned by the government in 2006, however, it was surrounded by a forest of high-rise buildings, and Hong Kong was one of the most densely populated cities in the world. That this site was never overrun and consumed by the city's commercial building boom, means that this Victorian-era compound, with its parade ground and prison yard, is a rare oasis of public space. When Herzog & de Meuron was approached by the Hong Kong Jockey Club in 2006 to work with them on the revitalisation of this special site and to repurpose it into the Tai Kwun cultural centre while preserving its historic colonial elements, we immediately saw the huge potential this site has for Hong Kong.

Long before Herzog & de Meuron was identified with such signature projects as the Tate Modern in London or the Elbphilharmonie in Hamburg, we had embraced the creative reuse of existing space or material that pays respect to its past while adapting it to contemporary needs. We welcome the restrictions this approach imposes to fuel and inspire our architecture, and at the same time to anchor the projects in their respective contexts. With world resources becoming ever scarcer, the concept of 'reduce, reuse, recycle' becomes a significant departure from the tabula-rasa approach to architectural innovation in which old buildings and entire neighbourhoods are simply demolished and completely rebuilt with modern structures.

In Hong Kong, this is still a very new approach to architecture and it was our goal with this project to set a new standard in historic building conservation. The original buildings on site are of no great antiquity or architectural significance, yet are an important part of Hong Kong's history. The compound is defined and structured by two large courtyards: the Parade Ground and the Prison Yard. Our goal was to preserve the openness and distinct character of both and to reactivate them for public use as a new type of urban found space. These spaces will define the site physically and programmatically as places of gathering, cultural activities, leisure and respite.

With this in mind, the creative reuse concept of Tai Kwun, at the heart of the city but historically walled off from it, aimed at achieving an accessible but quiet public place for decompression, slowing down, education and exchange. The old buildings stay, supplemented by two new structures that complete the site development.

We carefully study what is there, what can be saved and reused, what makes sense to be incorporated. It is the opposite of a clean slate. This is the idea of revitalisation, which goes beyond the mere built environment. It is also necessary to think the project through on a programmatic level – that is, how the site is intended to be used. Only then can a building or building complex be successfully reactivated. Lastly it is also important that the newly built, while being informed by the existing, clearly states that it is of today and not a reconstruction or simulation of the past.

Herzog & de Meuron,
Tai Kwun centre for
heritage and arts,
Hong Kong,
2018

The two new grey buildings blend
into the fabric of the existing
Central Police Station Compound
in Hong Kong.

The historic police headquarters and barracks blocks surround the Parade Ground, which allows ample space for public social life, events, restaurants and retail outlets, as well as cultural and educational events. The Prison Yard adds space for cultural programming. Here the two new buildings frame this newly opened-up public space like bookends, but instead of blocking the accessibility to the central courtyard, the buildings cantilever, or float, over the historic grounds. Rather than becoming an obstacle for the circulation through the site, the two floating buildings offer an attractive space beneath them, protected from rain and shine, that can be programmed in many different ways (movie nights, lectures, concerts, theatre and other performances). They expand the new arts and culture space throughout the site by introducing new unexpected and protected outdoor spaces. The colonial buildings on the historic compound of the former police station and prison often offer buffer spaces between the exterior and the interior – loggias and patios, covered balconies, partially covered courtyards.

In a way we continue this heritage by creating spaces that blur the boundaries between interior and exterior space. Like the wide laundry steps (on the site of the prison laundry) under the new JC Cube building, where the exterior facades of the adjacent historic prison buildings form the 'interior' walls of this impromptu outdoor auditorium space, a fascinating play between exterior and interior activates the in-between in an interesting way. The steps also serve as casual or performance seating.

Here the two new buildings frame this newly opened-up public space like bookends, but instead of blocking the accessibility, the buildings float over the historic grounds

The cantilever of the JC Cube building allows the structure to float over the Tai Kwun's existing historic site.

The cast aluminium facade uses a masonry interlocking principle for scale and proportion. This assembly strengthens the connections for structural stability and echoes the masonry units used in the existing structures.

One way we have honoured the marriage of old and new is through the use of new materials that are clearly distinct and contemporary, but which speak to the materiality of the historic buildings

acing the Challenges of a Historic Context

/hile the historic context defined the project
onceptually, it also presented problems. The site sits
 an extremely tight space, in the heart of a very active
ty surrounded by narrow streets on all four sides.
his made it highly challenging from a logistical and
lanning point of view. All interventions and insertions
ad to be carefully planned and executed. With three
fferent ground levels and a prison wall around, the
te was hard to navigate and access. After all, with
at historically significant prison wall, the site was
ot originally meant to serve as an open public space.
/hile we retained the wall around the site, we added
 few new precise openings in it and introduced a new
ootbridge that connected to the famous Hong Kong
lid-Levels escalator system to give direct access to the
arade ground from this important circulation vein. In
ddition, we carefully inserted new circulation paths
iroughout the site, new stairs and new lifts that link the
arade ground with the old prison yard.

One way we have honoured the marriage of old
nd new is through the use of new materials that are
early distinct and contemporary, but which speak to
ie materiality of the historic buildings. For example, all
sible concrete surfaces are treated with a needle gun
 achieve a texture that establishes a dialogue with the
irface of the historic granite blocks used throughout
ie site. Needle gunning the concrete also gives it a
orous look and makes it a sensual surface. People like
 touch it, and it is visually softer than untreated out-of-
rm concrete.

Likewise, the recycled aluminium facade of both new
buildings is rough cast, giving the aluminium blocks
a crafted look and feel, like masonry blocks or bricks.
The blocks have this inherent physical material quality
that could never be achieved with folded sheet metal,
for example. And they establish a dialogue with the
surrounding historically very significant prison wall
with its large granite blocks, yet they are still much
lighter and able to fulfil the performance needs of the
two new buildings.

Designing an Interlocking Facade System

We always develop our details in a creative and
constructive dialogue with the manufacturing industry.
In the case of the facade this process began with the
aluminium casting industry located in nearby Shenzhen.
Over a long period of research and trial-and-error, the
casting process for the blocks was developed from
simple sand casting to a more precise die-casting
method. It was rewarding to work with an industry that
typically produces dies for casting motor blocks or car
wheels. This process also triggered the idea of casting
only one block that is then simply cut to achieve the
different apertures needed.

The connection and structural system of the facade
is designed based on an interlocking principle. Rows of
perforated blocks interlock to create a stiff frame able
to span the distance while being fixed directly to the
main structural steel frame, eliminating the need for
a subframe. The four aperture sizes provide different
levels of porosity, allowing various intensities of light

e facade blocks are produced
m one mould. The variation is
eated through cutting each cast
ce at different depths. These
pths are determined using
nctional and environmental
quirements of the uses within
e building.

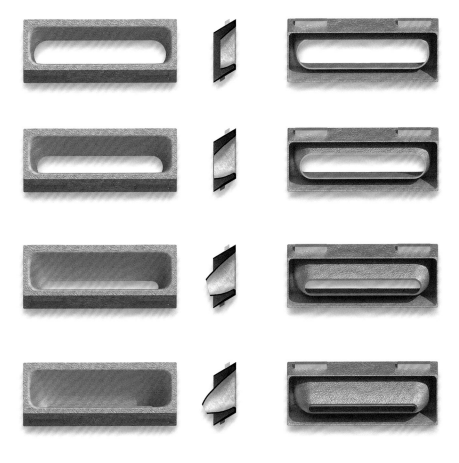

The actual cut of each block
had to react to the geometry
of the adjacent block,
which resulted in an interesting
irregular cutting line

Facade blocks are cut into two separate
planes to form the corner detail.

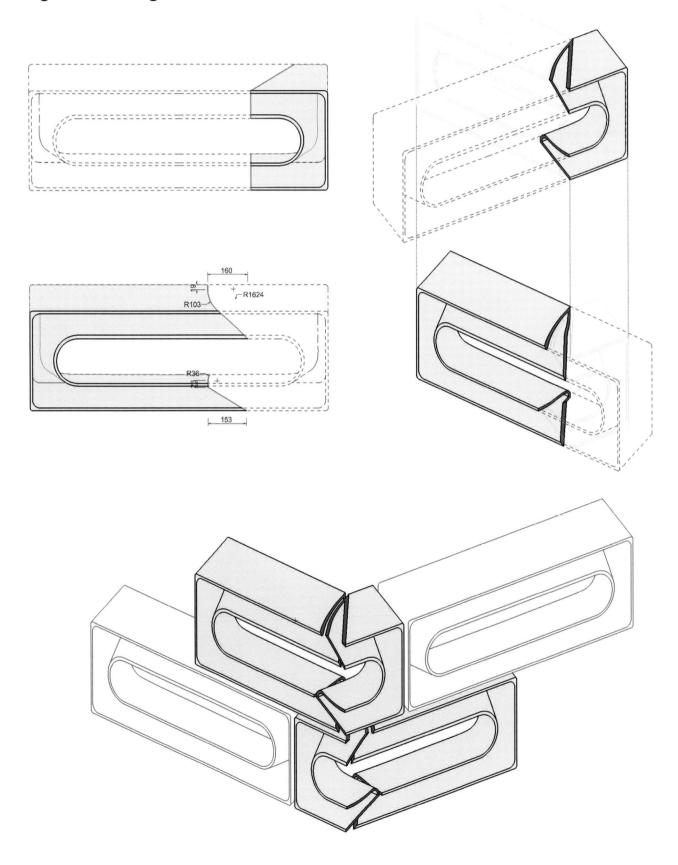

enter in order to respond to the specific functional requirements of the type of interior programme behind them, and giving a textured variety in appearance. Together, the system acts as a sun and rain screen, obscures mechanical equipment from view, but is also porous enough to allow adequate air circulation and views to the outside when desired. Its tactile and porous surface is designed to be experienced from both the inside and the outside. On the outside, its textured surface helps to reduce reflectivity and glare during the daytime. At night, light emitted from the building will be partially screened, expressing life of the activities within without creating heavy light pollution.

An interesting detail is the way the building's corners join together rather than meet at a sharp 90-degree angle. The interlocking aspect of the corner detail is crucial. Corners are important moments in a facade and rather than simply solving it with a mitre, where the two facades would be literally cut into two separate planes,

our primary interest was much more in 'knitting' the facade around the corner; to strengthen the corner rather than weaken it. The actual cut of each block had to react to the geometry of the adjacent block, which resulted in an interesting irregular cutting line. But it was also impossible to match the geometries of the two adjacent blocks completely, and this slight imperfection makes the corner even stronger. It adds an aspect of craftsmanship, and, like in the historic buildings where corners are often also treated in a special way, it creates a unique moment with the tools and methods of today.

Means and Ends

The design tools used on this facade were 3D-modelling software, scripting protocols, 5-axis milling machines, and 1:1 models made out of cardboard, Styrofoam, high-density foam and aluminium. The computer makes these solutions relatively straightforward, and why not use the advantages of a CAD/CAM production process, if it ultimately results in a more interesting detail? Details like this sit at the crossroads of analogue and digital, which is something Herzog & de Meuron is very interested in. That said, digital design and fabrication methods are very powerful tools but should not overpower the sensual and spatial qualities of the built architecture. The German words *Werkzeug* and *Selbstzweck* describe this relationship and our understanding of how to use digital technologies in the design process very well: digital technologies are a *Werkzeug* (tool) and should not become a *Selbstzweck* (an end in itself). ⅅ

above: A close-up detail of the corner unit prototype, produced in 2011, shows that the units do not resolve in a continuous manner. This is due to two different geometries colliding revealing the fabrication method.

left: As the different corner units assemble, they produce a visually intricate corner condition. The corner reveals the folded sheet-metal interior which contrasts with the block-shaped unit exterior.

BEYOND THE AVANT-GARDE

THE MATERIALITY OF ARCHITECTURE AND ITS IMPACT

Antoine Picon

AJ Rosales,
Thermodynamic energies
at a diving stadium
for the Tokyo 2020 Olympics,
2015

A thermodynamically driven exploration combining natural site cooling and an adjustable multi-layer thermal balloon structure over the main amphitheatre.

In the last 25 years, since the beginning of the 'first digital turn' in architecture, the imperative towards sustainability and the preoccupations of the virtual vanguard have seldom been bedfellows. Antoine Picon, Harvard Professor of the History of Architecture and Technology, sees some green shoots in the post-digital world.

TC Howard,
Climatron,
St Louis,
Missouri,
1960

opposite: The geodesic-domed greenhouse is clearly indebted to Buckminster Fuller's environmental concerns.

Philippe Rahm architectes,
Convective Apartment,
Hamburg, Germany,
2010

below: Rahm's work illustrates the rising importance of environmental factors in architecture. Thermal exchanges, gradients of temperature and humidity – illustrated through colour on this interior view – are becoming as important as structural considerations

For a little over 25 years, digital avant-gardes have been announcing a profound revolution in the foundations and practice of the architectural discipline. Twenty-five years is a long period of time, and it should be no surprise that the alleged content of this revolution has varied considerably between the dawn of computer-aided architecture in the mid-1990s and the present day. Whereas form and its animation occupied a privileged position in the first writings and experiments dealing with the perspectives opened up by digital technologies in architecture, digital fabrication is playing a much more important role in today's discourse and practice. In recent years, issues related to the relationship between coding and design and above all speculations regarding the mobilisation of artificial intelligence in architecture have also gained momentum.

Strangely, given its crucial importance in our anxious and endangered contemporary world, climate change has not been very present in this story, as if issues of thermal exchanges, grey energy and rising waters were peripheral to the revolution announced by digital avant-gardes, including the present-day advocates of artificial intelligence. In schools of architecture, this estrangement is easy to measure. Proponents of algorithmic manipulations and supporters of a resilient and frugal architecture, investigators of machine vision procedures and users of computer fluid dynamics (CFD) software, have limited interactions. This situation is in complete contrast with the close association between a keen interest for computers and environmental concerns that characterised forerunners of digital culture like Buckminster Fuller – concerns epitomised by projects inspired by his work such as the Climatron (1960, designed by TC Howard) in St Louis, Missouri.

There is an urgent need to connect intimately these two key domains of design, and such a connection is expected by the public at large. The main point is that an examination of what environmental concerns and climate change are currently doing to architecture might actually help throw some light on the complex question of the real nature of the digital revolution in architecture, beyond the successive crazes of digital avant-gardes. For the digital has clearly contributed to changing the way the discipline is understood and practised, but not necessarily in the terms usually employed to characterise this change. Instead of evoking dimensions such as the 'non-standard', 'Parametricism' or 'Discretism', it is possible to refer to the notion of materiality and argue that, alongside the rise of environmental concerns, the digital is part of a global shift in the materiality of architecture.[1] Unpacking what this means in concrete terms should also lead to a better understanding of what the impact of digital architecture is truly about.

THE ENVIRONMENTAL TURNING POINT IN ARCHITECTURE

The first consequence of the rise of environmental concerns has been a profound shift in the set of physical phenomena that architecture has to take into account, as well as in their respective importance. Architects like Philippe Rahm have for instance stressed the increasing attention paid to temperature gradients that used to be only marginally considered by modernist and post-modern architecture, while others such as Iñaki Ábalos have contrasted the rising importance of thermodynamic behaviour as opposed to traditional structural factors.[2] The very notion of material is also evolving. It now encompasses dimensions such as embodied energy and reuse that were generally neglected by designers in the past. This series of transformations is by no means univocal; it is permeated with contradictions. The growing concern for material reuse is for instance contemporary with the spread of composite materials, which are generally difficult to recycle properly. Despite these contradictions, a possible way to make sense of what is happening before our eyes is to consider that the physical world to which architecture refers has become different from the one to which former generations of designers used to refer. More accurately, it is the relationship between designers and the physical world that has changed. By suggesting that they should pay more attention to temperatures, energy exchanges, bio-sourcing and recycling procedures than they did in the past, designers contribute to altering the relationship between all those who inhabit their buildings and the physical world that surrounds them.

A second major lesson to be drawn from this shift concerns the link it has with emergent forms of subjectivity. The search for an environmentally conscious architecture evidently has to do with a recognition of the fact that we have entered a new era marked by a dramatically increased human footprint – the Anthropocene – and this is inextricably linked to a series of transformations regarding the way human beings see themselves in relation to an endangered world that they should preserve. The change in the way we understand and experience what it is to be human is not only a matter of self-perception. It involves new attitudes and behaviours such as the frugality advocated by so many environmental activists.

MATERIALITY AS A RELATIONSHIP

Materiality can be interpreted as the relationship that humans have with the physical world at a given moment in history and in a given society.[3] Although it may initially appear purely objective, independent of science, technology and culture, materiality is to a certain extent a construct that depends on the prevailing knowledge and modes of action on the physical world as well as on the current beliefs, economy and politics. Envisaged from that perspective, materiality is inseparable from the way humans understand themselves through the lens of their relationship with their physical environment.

Architecture plays an important role in this relationship. Indeed, the discipline is based on the assumption that buildings, these eminently material objects, can enter into an intimate relationship with humans, fulfil their needs, induce sensations, move them, and thus reveal some key features of the human condition. To inhabit or to dwell means precisely to define oneself partially through this intimate relation with objects made of earth, brick, stone, steel or concrete, which reveals something about the body and mind. Architecture is ultimately about inhabiting in the full sense of the term, from the practicality of sheltering to the impressions and feelings that contribute to structuring the mental sphere.

THE DIGITAL AND THE MATERIAL

Returning now to the digital, a very similar case can be made. Beyond its formal affectations and the current fascination exerted by robots or artificial intelligence algorithms on so many of its proponents, it is worth remembering that digital architecture goes hand in hand with a profound reshaping of our experience and understanding of the physical world, as well as with a significant transformation of contemporary subjectivity. The experiential dimension is especially important. Indeed, digital technologies have transformed the way humans see, hear and touch. We can no longer see without being decisively influenced by digital cameras. We listen to compressed digital files, and we wear perfumes that have been synthesised with the aid of sophisticated software that allows for the combination of fragrances in the same way that designers juggle with forms and colours using graphics programs. The list of ways in which the human relationship to the physical world has been transformed by the digital is simply astonishing.

An abundance of literature has been devoted to the new understanding of the human in relation to the rise of digital technologies. Are humans becoming cyborgs through their more and more intimate connection with technology? Will cyborgs still be human, or will they epitomise the first stage of a post-human condition at the intersection of biology and technology? Rather than the spectacular hybrids of flesh and machine imagined by Hollywood, cyborgs should perhaps be envisaged as complex networked ecologies that blur the distinction between the self and its environment and make obsolete the notion of a clear-cut boundary between subjective interiority and a purely objective exterior. Advocates of this latter view often make reference to the work of the late cyberneticist Gregory Bateson or to the conceptual framework laid out by the philosopher Gilles Deleuze.[4]

University of Tasmania and Fologram,
Construction of the new K block of the Royal Hobart Hospital,
Hobart, Australia,
2018

A holographic model guides the workers in laying the bricks for a complex feature wall. The cyborg condition equally affects designers, workers and inhabitants.

University of Tasmania and Fologram, Bricklaying workshop,
University of Tasmania,
Launceston, Australia,
2018

Augmented reality is emblematic of the increasing hybridisation of atoms and bits of information that defines contemporary materiality, the materiality of architecture.

Institute for Computational Design and Construction (ICD) and Institute for Building Structures and Structural Design (ITKE),
ICD/ITKE Research Pavilion 2016-17 (detail),
University of Stuttgart, Germany,
2017

opposite left: In approaches such as material computation, epitomised by the work led by Achim Menges at the Stuttgart Institute for Computational Design and Construction, the digital and the material dimensions are inseparable from one another.

Herzog & de Meuron,
de Young Museum,
San Francisco, California,
2005

opposite right: The envelope of the de Young Museum illustrates the blurring between senses, and in particular between vision and touch, that characterises large swaths of contemporary ornamental practices.

The development of digital architecture bears the mark of s double evolution. Digital designers have been fascinated some key characteristics of the new physical world that nfolding before our eyes, such as the blurring of matter d computation invoked by proponents of 'material mputation' such as architects and researchers Achim enges and Jenny Sabin, or the importance accorded to listic properties like emergence.[5] They have explored possibilities offered by the different sensorium that emerging in relation to our changing experience of physical world, and as a testimony to the profound nsformation of subjectivity that is taking place today. e shift in visual categories that has led to the progressive andonment of the perspectival frame and to new nnections between vision and touch is among the ections taken by this quest for new sensory and perceptual egories. The so-called 'return' of ornament appears as one the most striking architectural consequences of the joint olution of the experience and understanding of the ysical world and of subjectivity. Indeed, contemporary nament is often based on the apparent convergence tween the visual and the tactile; its affective character ems to suggest that the distinction between subject and ject is no longer operative.

At another level, digital architecture has echoed a series of epistemological transformations such as the radical questioning of the traditional distinction between deep structures and the superficial layer, analogous to a skin, that was supposed to cover them. This has led to a crisis of tectonics and more generally to the critical re-examination of modes of articulation and assemblages. Ornament, often indistinguishable from structure, appears again as a revealing symptom of this crisis.

Instead of focusing on the successive enthusiasms and buzzwords that digital avant-gardes have used to propel themselves into the limelight, it might be more productive to step back in order to consider these more fundamental changes in the relationship between humans and the material world, a changing relationship linked to new forms of subjectivity. In other words, digital design has been expressing a shift in the materiality of architecture in a manner more consistent than what is usually assumed by theorists and critics. How should we build in an inherently unstable and fluid world? How do we inhabit as cyborgs deprived of the spatial ideals presupposed by modernism and with different sensory and perceptive habitus? These questions are perhaps what matters the most today. Answering them might prove crucial if we want to understand the true impact of architecture in the post-digital age.

In order to reach this understanding, we must recognise that there are not two physical worlds and two sorts of materiality stemming from the relationship humans have with them. Advocates of the environment and digital designers are actually exploring the same world: a world characterised by its fluidity, its strong material dimension (materials having become one of the new frontiers of design, whether they be bio-sourced or digitally produced); a world of full of instabilities, and in a perpetual state of emergence. In such a world, the envelopes or skins of buildings and the materials that these envelopes are made of are often more important than their inner structure. Indeed, everything seems about flow and exchange, thermal energy, light or electronic contents.

TOWARDS AN ECOLOGICAL ARCHITECTURE

Environmental and digital designs share a renewed interest in the bodies of the occupants of buildings. Both are actually breaking away from the modernist approach of the human body as a clearly bounded entity entirely distinct from its surroundings. It is worth noting at this stage that cyborg or networked forms of subjectivity are equally useful for the purposes of rethinking the human status in relation to the rise of digital technologies and in the age of climate change. Both imply that to be human is synonymous with being dependent upon an inextricably technological and natural environment – science and technology studies often evoke a 'techno-nature' – that cannot be considered as a mere exterior.

Because it bridges domains usually separated by a marked gap, the new design approach advocated here at the intersection of digital and environmental concerns could truly merit being called ecological. Indeed, it connects humans to the both dense and fluid networks that constitute today's techno-nature. It is about the environment envisaged in the broadest possible sense. It is about how humans are inseparable from this complex environment, how materiality, the materiality of architecture mediates their relation to it.

Gramazio Kohler Research,
Design and Robotic Fabrication
of Jammed Architectural Structures,
ETH, Zurich, Switzerland,
2015-19

top: An investigation into the articulation of advanced robotic fabrication and a quest for sustainability based on the use of low-grade building materials.

above: With remarkable precision, forms arise literally from rubble.

ecoLogicStudio,
SuperTree (detail),
ZKM, Karlsruhe, Germany,
2018

Attempting to repurpose the tree to optimise its operations, the project
blurs the distinction between the natural and the artificial, the organic and
the digital. It clearly belongs to the realm of contemporary 'techno-nature'.

To produce an impactful ecological architecture today probably requires an ability to relate the new elements and techniques of architecture – certainly not the floors, walls and ceilings staged by Rem Koolhaas for the 2014 Venice Biennale, but machine-learning procedures or interior climates – to the human body and mind, just like the Vitruvian tradition grounded proportions on the measures of men and women.[6] Elements and techniques should not be arbitrary or floating in the abstract, but should contribute to the concrete articulation of design strategies with inhabiting or dwelling concerns. A major challenge lies in recognising that inhabiting or dwelling is both eminently local (to live in a specific place and building) and global, at the scale of the planet. This is what digital technologies and climate change force us to consider head on because of their ubiquity. In his often-quoted text 'Building Dwelling Thinking' (originally published in German in 1954), the philosopher Martin Heidegger foresaw this profoundly transcalar character.[7] In other words, how is design to be material at these very different scales – the close-by that can be touched by extending the arm, and the far-away to which we are connected in so many ways?

This should lead to enquiries regarding the sense in which architecture can be exemplary today, beyond the seduction of digital virtuosity or environmental moralism, and above all far away from the superficial glamour of star-projects. What is a meaningful precedent and what can serve as model? Because of its newness and implicit presentism, digital architecture had forgotten this fundamental question. As for environmentally conscious design, it tends to reduce the question to the implementation of atemporal principles. Combining digital literacy with environmental consciousness may be one of the ways to rebuild the architectural discipline or rather to reconcile it with its own historicity.[8] ∆

Notes
1. On these notions, see for instance: Frédéric Migayrou and Zeynep Mennan (eds), *Architectures non standard*, Éditions du Centre Pompidou (Paris), 2003; Patrik Schumacher, *Autopoiesis: I. A New Agenda for Architecture* and *II. A New Framework for Architecture*, John Wiley & Sons (Chichester), 2011 and 2012; and Mario Carpo, *The Second Digital Turn: Design Beyond Intelligence*, The MIT Press (Cambridge, MA), 2017.
2. Philippe Rahm, *Le Jardin Météorologique et autres constructions climatiques*, Éditions B2 (Paris), 2019; Iñaki Abalos and Renata Sentkiewicz, *Essays on Thermodynamics: Architecture and Beauty*, Actar (Barcelona), 2015.
3. See Antoine Picon, *La Matérialité de l'architecture*, Parenthèses (Marseilles), 2018.
4. See for instance William J Mitchell, *Me++: The Cyborg Self and the Networked City*, The MIT Press (Cambridge, MA), 2003.
5. Achim Menges (ed), ∆ *Material Computation: Higher Integration in Morphogenetic Design*, March/April (no 2), 2012; Jenny E Sabin and Peter Lloyd Jones, *LabStudio: Design Research Between Architecture and Biology*, Routledge (New York), 2018.
6. Rem Koolhaas (ed), *Elements of Architecture*, Taschen (Cologne), 2018; Hanno Walter Kruft, *A History of Architectural Theory: From Vitruvius to the Present*, Princeton Architectural Press (New York), 1994.
7. Martin Heidegger, 'Building, Dwelling, Thinking' (1954), in *Poetry, Language, Thought*, trans Albert Hofstadter, Harper and Row (New York), 1971, pp 145–61.
8. The author would like to thank Hina Jamelle and Hanan Kataw for their suggestions regarding the images accompanying this article.

Ben van Berkel

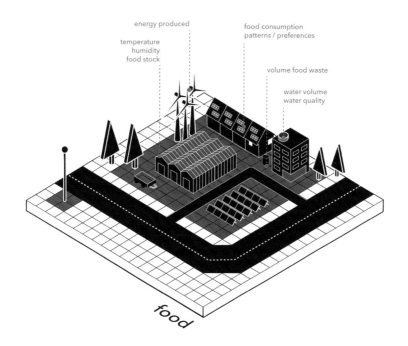

energy produced

temperature
humidity
food stock

food consumption
patterns / preferences

volume food waste

water volume
water quality

food

UNSense, 100 Homes,
Brainport Smart District,
Helmond,
The Netherlands,
2019-

Example of the 'Circular Urban Farming' physical
layer. The collection of data enables an increase in
operational efficiency, the reduction of negative
impacts such as CO_2 emissions, and new forms of
collective, community-scale ownership.

ARCHITECTU
IMPACT OF TH
INDUSTRIAL

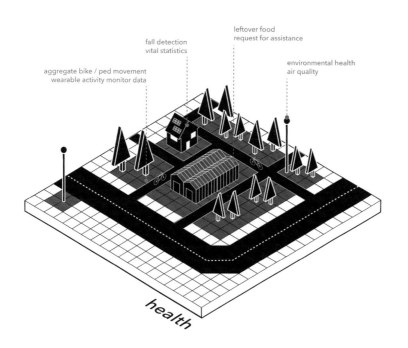

fall detection
vital statistics

leftover food
request for assistance

aggregate bike / ped movement
wearable activity monitor data

environmental health
air quality

health

Example of the 'Healthy Environment' physical
layer. While technology is often framed as
antagonistic to public life, 100 Homes seeks to test
if, when used in the right way, it can reinvigorate
public space and provide new opportunities for
interaction and public engagement.

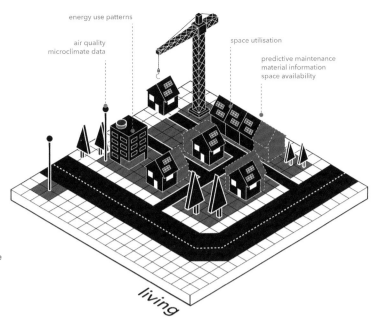

energy use patterns

air quality
microclimate data

space utilisation

predictive maintenance
material information
space availability

living

Example of the 'Adaptive Architecture' physical layer.
Innovations in sensor technologies and manufacturing enable
a rethinking of the ways in which we construct and inhabit
buildings. UNSense seeks to implement technologies in the
home that allow us to live better lives at a lower cost.

RE AND THE
E FOURTH
REVOLUTION

Example of the 'Mobility Hub' physical
layer. A mobility hub that serves as the
central link between many transportation
modalities, by layering social functions
it becomes a place for gathering,
interaction and encounter.

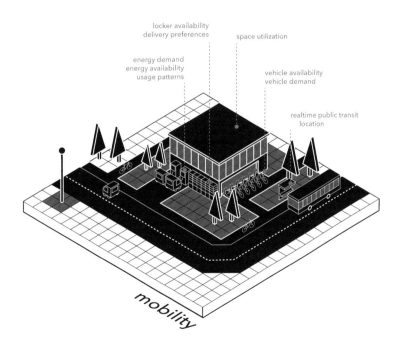

locker availability
delivery preferences

space utilization

energy demand
energy availability
usage patterns

vehicle availability
vehicle demand

realtime public transit
location

mobility

UNStudio and UNSense founder **Ben van Berkel** explains the post-digital symbiotic role that disruptive, embedded data technologies can have in the technologies architects use to design, enabling them to produce more and more tailored buildings that are informed by accurate fed-back information. Here he uses one of UNSense's housing schemes as an example.

When we speak of the role of the digital within the discipline of architecture, it is perhaps important to first distinguish between the digital tools we use during the design process (computational design tools), new construction techniques (3D printing and robotics) and the advanced digital applications that are fast becoming an integrated part of our buildings, cities and lives today ('disruptive technologies').

With computational design, designers can save a great deal of time and calculation by feeding variables into the tool, which then produces a number of iterations that architects can further tweak in order to optimise the outcome. A common misconception about computational, or parametric, design, is that it is automatically associated with pattern-making, or with a certain style of architecture. But this is in fact not the case. Aesthetic choices are based on trends, not on the tools we use to design. One inherent danger, however, is that computational design can result in overly complex form-making for its own sake, or merely for visual impact. But when used to find the best solutions for a given set of highly varied parameters – both geometric and non-geometric – computational modelling can be guided to produce highly refined and performative solutions; solutions that are often invisible and that directly relate to how the building performs and is experienced.

New technologies and techniques for material assembly also present unprecedented possibilities for designers with respect to material choices, form finding, speed of construction and circularity.

Disruptive technologies, on the other hand, are more often associated with cultural impact. Business models such as Airbnb and Uber have considerably expanded choice and proved financially beneficial to the consumer. But they are also often accused of having a negative effect on their host cities. Airbnb, for example, has proved unpopular with residents who suddenly find their neighbours to be a steady stream of – often noisy – tourists. Likewise, there is currently a backlash in some cities against the number of much-needed homes being purchased for rent on such platforms – and as such adding to a local housing crisis.

However, within the discipline of architecture, designers can now combine design thinking and data technology to create more human-centric cities and buildings. The data that new technologies can gather can be appropriated to inform and improve design with respect to user behaviour. As such, these technologies make possible the quantification of human flows and behaviours in the built environment, thereby providing new parameters for use during the design process. Such data sets, alongside new technologies such as

...nsors, drones or autonomous vehicles, also enable designers
...propose new solutions for specific urban challenges such
...safety or mobility. In addition, new technologies allow
...e development of sensor-based environments that respond,
...arn and adjust to users' daily activities, thereby taking smart
...ildings towards responsive architecture through systems
...at offer intuitive control and personalisation of space.

...It is these advanced digital applications that have
...cessitated the most significant expansion to the discipline
...architecture in recent years. The fourth industrial
...volution, with the explosiveness of its development and
...e disruptiveness of its technologies, has brought about a
...ndition in which it has become imperative for architects to
...oaden their understanding and approach to both practice
...d the design of cities and buildings.

UNSense,
100 Homes,
Brainport Smart District,
Helmond,
The Netherlands,
2019-

100 Homes will test new equal data-exchange models at the
neighbourhood level. By integrating technology into homes,
cars and public spaces, the aim is to validate how daily
activities (grocery shopping, cooking, household chores)
can be made easier, while costs can be saved.

The Digital Imprint

What do we mean when we speak of the 'impact' of
architecture with respect to the advent of digital technologies?
In the late 1990s and into the first decade of the 21st century,
computational design tools radically changed the way we
produced architecture and design. At the same time, an
iconic design approach was widely adopted that primarily
emphasised the brand value of buildings and was largely based
on a culture of visual impact; on the 'image' of architecture.
However, following the financial crisis of 2008, most clients
began to reject the monofunctional emphasis of visual impact
and began to demand highly performative, sustainable,
human-centric, technology-driven, safer and healthier
buildings. Buildings were now required to impact on a level of
multiple parameter performance. Indeed, this extended beyond
site boundaries to include consideration of the impact of a
building on its immediate surroundings and the host city as a
whole. What would the building give back to the city, and to
the people of the city?

In the intervening years, disruptive technologies have begun
to take centre stage, the impact of which on the discipline of
architecture – although perhaps not initially overtly apparent –
is now fast emerging. The societal impact of these technologies
since they first emerged is widely documented; however, the
potential use (and value) of the data that forms their backbone

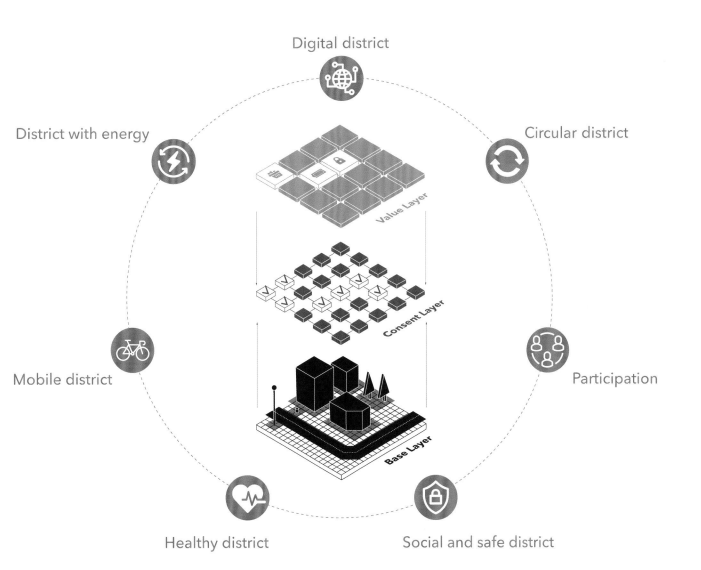

Digital district

District with energy

Circular district

Mobile district

Participation

Healthy district

Social and safe district

New technologies allow
the development of sensor-
based environments that
respond, learn and adjust
to users' daily activities

The project can be understood in three layers: the physical layer (built environment with sensors); data layer (urban data platform); and value layer (services).

and key product has only recently begun to affect the built environment. And it is here that the practice of architecture has faced its most recent and challenging expansion.

Most contemporary architecture firms employ experienced parametric designers and building information modelling (BIM) experts, but they do not yet have the resources or expertise to analyse data, nor to use it to inform design. Increasingly, however, the capacity to integrate technology or user experience (UX) into the built environment from the initial design stages is becoming a requirement, as is the use of advanced technological systems as the key drivers of a solution-based design. This means that formerly siloed professions now need to overlap, and collaboration with other disciplines has become paramount for architects.

It is for this reason that in 2018 UNSense was founded. As a subsidiary company to UNStudio, UNSense takes an independent position that enables it to think critically about technologies and give form to the role designers and architects should take in these united realities. UNSense currently comprises a team of architects, interaction designers, software developers, researchers and futurists who form collaborations with academic experts, strategic commercial partners, and local citizens and entrepreneurs to design for the mixed reality of connective technologies and spatial design.

Architects of course design not only to accommodate, but to enhance how people live. In order to do this adequately they have to respond to (and take advantage of) any societal or technological changes that may occur on a large scale. As such, disruptive technologies, along with the data that underlies them, present not only design challenges for architects, but also ethical quandaries: if we use data to inform design, we enter the political arena.

One current UNSense project that illustrates both the challenges and opportunities presented by these new realities is the 100 Homes real-life test environment that is currently being developed for the Brainport Smart District in Helmond, the Netherlands. Within that masterplan, an adaptive neighbourhood of 100 houses will be built and an urban data platform will be developed to host services related to housing, energy, mobility and health.

The 100 Homes project is conceived as a 'living lab' – a constantly evolving innovative environment where data and technology are applied at a neighbourhood level to benefit the residents both socially and economically. With the first residents scheduled to move in by 2022, the goal is to develop intelligent services that connect and adapt to needs and consumption habits, enabling basic services to become manageable and fixed costs to be reduced, thus resulting in an increase of (net) income for the residents. However, the nature of such an intelligent, learning, adaptive urban district is that precise needs and related services cannot be determined in advance. These will need to be developed in collaboration with the residents and understood through their use of the space.

The project is therefore investigating an alternative new model for equal data exchange. The current dominant data-based business model relies on data that consumers and small companies – at times unwittingly – provide to technology companies in exchange for free services: a structure from which only the tech companies profit.

The profession needs to look beyond 'bricks and mortar'; to expand its knowledge and skills base to be in a position to respond to and incorporate the new technologies causing cultural impact globally

Use case: Food. The physical, data and value layers are interconnected via the exchange of data in the domains of food. The data layer facilitates consent and equal exchange, meaning that the value layer benefits all stakeholders.

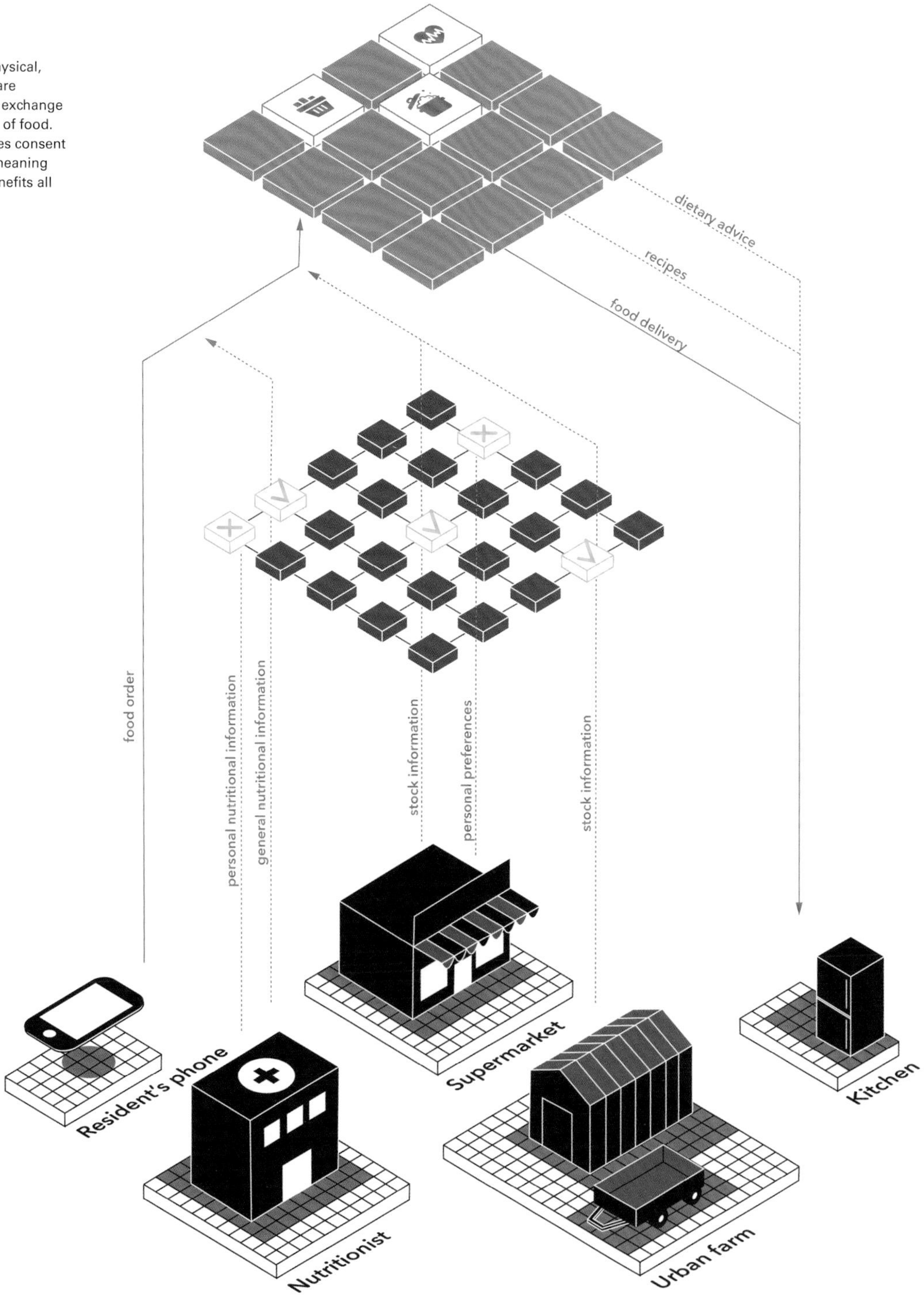

dietary advice

recipes

food delivery

food order

personal nutritional information

general nutritional information

stock information

personal preferences

stock information

Resident's phone

Nutritionist

Supermarket

Urban farm

Kitchen

he urban data platform at Brainport Smart District, owever, will operate on a principle of equal exchange and ser consent, meaning that data ownership is controlled y the end user, who maintains complete control of which ata is shared and with whom. A small-scale living lab ich as the 100 Homes project can therefore offer an pportunity to validate innovative design solutions and test their scalability.

elevant Expansion

ince the early 2000s, the architecture and construction idustries have faced the urgency – and have developed rategies, solutions and new materials – to tackle issues lated to climate change. However, if they are to remain relevant and achieve lasting impact, designers can no longer afford to perceive digital technologies merely as tools for the physical production of architecture. Instead, the profession needs to look beyond 'bricks and mortar'; to expand its knowledge and skills base to be in a position to respond to and incorporate the new technologies causing cultural impact globally. To achieve this, architects need to emerge from a silo mentality and forge collaborations with experts in other fields. Only in this way will it be possible to face head-on the challenges (and opportunities) these technologies present, and to ensure that the discipline of architecture remains relevant and is prepared for whatever future developments may ensue. ⌂

se case: Energy. Residents can
t to provide segments of their
ersonal data to third parties in
xchange for energy-use cost
vings, in which equal exchange
a key principle.

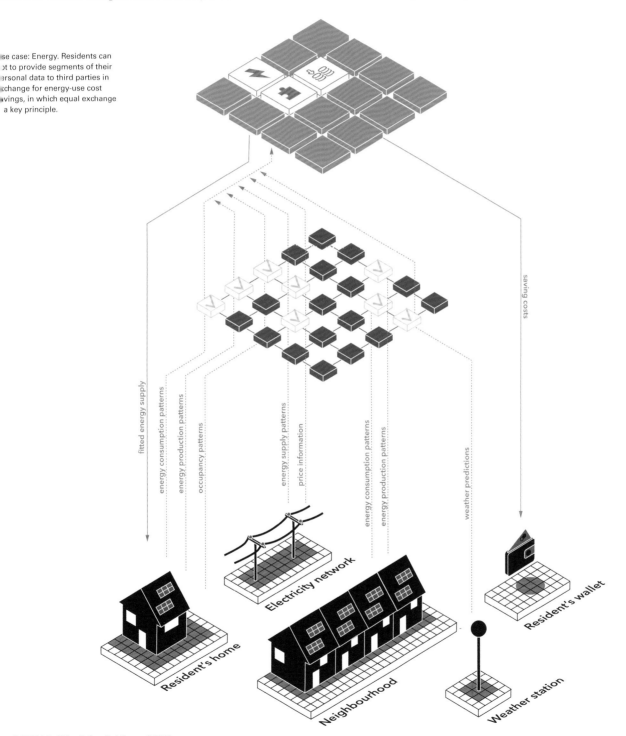

THE IMPACT OF THE DIGITAL ON BIGG-NESS

A Word from ⵏ Editor Neil Spiller

SIDE ONE
ONE **ALL THE PLACES OF THE WORLD**
TWO **ALONE**
THREE **HOME**
FOUR **HAIKU**
SIDE TWO
ONE **WELCOME**
TWO **GRAZIA**
THREE **MOONLIT**
FOUR **TO THE END**

(encore) Ensemble

Stefano Guzzetti: PIANO
Sara Meloni: VIOLIN
Giulia Dessy: VIOLA
Gianluca Pischedda: CELLO

CAT № **SR09LP**
manufactured in the eu

Isn't the act of drawing, as well as drawing itself about becoming rather than being? Isn't drawing the polar opposite of a photo? The latter stops time; whereas a drawing flows with it. Could we think of drawings as eddies on the surface of the stream of time? — **John Berger**[1]

Like all disciplines, the impact of the digital has changed the nature of graphic design and the ways in which one learns one's skills. You are more likely to see serried ranks of computers occupying graphic design studios today rather than typographers' blocks, photographic darkrooms, drawing boards, scalpels and photomechanical transfer machines. Often the computer has enabled a limited visual expression or created a ubiquity of images – a strange paradox for such a powerful machine. The same is mostly true in current architectural output.

One might argue that those who were trained before the virtual wave hit the creative coastline of architecture and graphic design, yet have adapted to its potential, have benefited from a greater possibility to develop a personal, signature way of working than those trained in a purely digital idiom. Today's students

Chris Bigg, album cover for Stefano Guzzetti's (encore) Ensemble, Stella Recordings, 2017

Bigg's cover for Italian electronic music composer Stefano Guzzetti brings together disparate objects, lines, splodges and representational techniques, letting the eye explore their correspondence yet also their differences like a series of musical notes making a visual composition.

STEFANO GUZZETTI

(encore) Ensemble

of both disciplines are digital natives. They think in, and hence their creative epistemologies are conceived in, the realm of the app, the algorithm, the 'cut and paste' equivalence of images and the Photoshop® tool bag – and this can often make work that is essentially self-similar. The signature of the architect or designer can get lost and not develop forward. A few students nowadays are becoming interested again in the mess and unpredictable techniques of the predigital, which are prone to mistakes and drippy, happy accidents.

British graphic designer Chris Bigg, perhaps best known for his expressive typography and calligraphy, has straddled both the analogue and the digital creative tide. His work has a sumptuous, instantly recognisable quality to it, no matter what guise it is in at a particular moment. He has interests in visualising music and sound. Experimentation and collaboration are essential to his working process, in which he sees sound and visuals as inseparable, where one informs the other. He has extensive experience in all areas of creative art directing, including design, photography and typography, and has worked in all aspects of music packaging creating cover art, special editions, posters, press ads, merchandising, production and moving image, as well as book and exhibition design. In 1987 he joined the late Vaughan Oliver at 23 Envelope (later v23). Their work for the 4AD record label, among others, has had a dramatic impact on graphic design.

Bigg remembers his first sightings of the 'great machine'. 'All very confusing; it was an ugly imposter, the craft of making work had to change, it hurt, it did my head in. I was just hitting my stride in expressing my vision with the analogue process, virtual folders and not plan chest drawers?'[2] The computer demanded different skills and ways of looking at things: 'The designer had to become everything: typesetter, courier, originator, the list goes on. I went to art college to be an artist not a typist, and that is how it felt – a keyboard for goodness sake! Give me a Rotring, French curve, scalpel and a ruler anyday.'

It is this synthesis of hand, eye and the virtual (in all its senses) that gives Bigg's work its undeniable power and quirky originality. It also relishes in Surrealist protocols and techniques, such as bringing together disparate forms and objects not normally seen in each other's company, and opening up the uncanny. 'After the initial wilderness years of coming to terms with digital technology I began to understand its benefits, for example communication. Making visuals for clients closer to how the finished piece might be, I could visualise exactly what I was thinking.' But he advises

Chris Bigg, album cover for The Breeders's *All Nerve*, 4AD, 2018

The humble and ubiquitous brick became the catalyst of this record sleeve. Seeing the creative opportunities in the most common of things is a trademark trait of Bigg's career. Photography by Martin Andersen.

some restraint as the hyperreal treatment of images in the digital realm can have the effect of removing their viscerality. 'I like to use the scanner as a creative tool and Photoshop has some excellent possibilities, but I use that with caution as it can get overdeveloped and therefore the original images can lose their original charm.'

The Art of the Accident

What Bigg and Oliver realised during those heady, post-punk days was that nothing needed to be complete, perfect or obsessed with purity of line or image. There is an ethereal, savage beauty and visual poetry in the haunting, hybridised work they produced. A beauty echoed in the music they were listening to and designing for. Each project always started with creative play, messing about to find a creative groove, out of which some extraordinary images would emerge: 'I start all my projects with analogue outcomes, be it mark-making, calligraphy, logo development. Then use InDesign as a layout tool for realising the project's outcome.'

Furniture manufacturers sometimes 'distress' recently made items to make them appear older than they are. This can be achieved with all manner of approaches, from incising, filing, dripping paint or filling to even firing a shotgun across a surface – all to appease a section of the buying public interested in the patina of supposed use. The aesthetic of distress is central to Bigg's modus operandi. He has developed many tactics to produce such effects and these are key to his distinctive output. His methods embrace chance in a restless search for the new, the extraordinary and the divine in the mundane, releasing the underlying art in the everyday. A ceaseless, emerging creativity powered by bringing together art, objects, photographs, line, smear and the unfocused in a festival of high-code and low-code uncanny juxtapositions. This shuffling of what we think we know visually instigates previously unimagined aesthetic conversations and fills us with a sense of newly discovered visual, typographic and calligraphic pleasures as our eyes flit inquisitively over them.

Bigg tries to instil this search for the new and the unexpected into his students at the University of Brighton: 'I reflect back to my practice. You need to take an idea to a computer. This is done by teaching via workshops, (no computers), experimental type, mark-making, collage, the art of the accident.' Creative dialogue and collaboration is also important in Bigg's creative universe, as is the questioning of all received 'wisdom': 'Talking to people face to face as a means of research makes your research personal. Pinterest is a virus – make your research unique! Students need to un-learn – school education is killing creativity. Collaboration and sharing ideas are essential. That would be great.'

Chris Bigg, Poster for Piroshka's *Brickbat* album, Bella Union, 2019

Overdrawing on typography, photographs and other drawings is used in this poster for modern punk band Piroshka to create an arresting collage at first looking like it has been defaced by a child. Here, graffiti and maverick composition come together. Design by Chris Bigg, photography by Martin Andersen and drawings by Mali.

'
I start all my projects with analogue outcomes, be it mark-making, calligraphy, logo development. Then use InDesign as a layout tool for realising the project's outcome
,

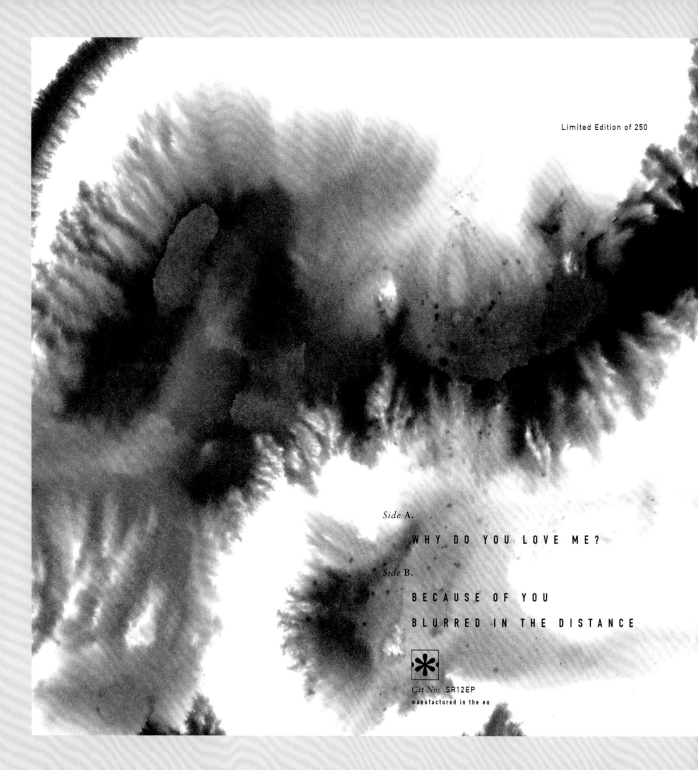

Side A.

WHY DO YOU LOVE ME?

Side B.

BECAUSE OF YOU

BLURRED IN THE DISTANCE

Cat No: SR12EP
manufactured in the eu

The choreography of chance and collaboration is one thing, but it is combined with the development over decades of Bigg's compositional 'eye'

Chris Bigg, album cover for Stefano Guzzetti's *Interludi*, Stella Recordings, 2019

Allowing chance into the creative equation and seizing its products and assimilating them into his graphic lexicon is a large facet of Bigg's designs.

Stefano Guzzetti
Interludi

The choreography of chance and collaboration is one thing, but it is combined with the development over decades of Bigg's compositional 'eye'. An eye honed in the white heat of the graphic design studio where every line and form is read, reread and adjusted to achieve the fine balance between the legibility of a piece relative to its calligraphic extravagance, for maximum effect.

All Nerve

Talking to Bigg is a joy – his frenetic roving eye, a twitching, nervy, excitable energy coupled with a softly spoken modesty and a dry wit. His personality comes across particularly in one recent album cover that is a microcosm of his general creative arc. In 2018 the rock band The Breeders, fronted by ex-Pixies Kim Deal,

released All Nerve after a 10-year hiatus. The studio album's artwork is a Bigg–Deal creative collaboration with a third partner Martin Andersen, also a graphic design tutor at Brighton University and also from the v23 stable.

Initially, Bigg worked almost synaesthetically, listening to the tracks, making marks and collaging them. Yet the catalytic form in the graphic language of the cover comes from his eye for the quotidian and invisible yet ubiquitous architectural staple, the brick. However, 'I thought … it might need something a bit singular, a bit stronger and iconic,' he explains. 'This brick has been in the garden for years. I've walked past it every day for years and years and I just thought,

ANALOGUE PROCESS

Chris Bigg 1987 - 2019

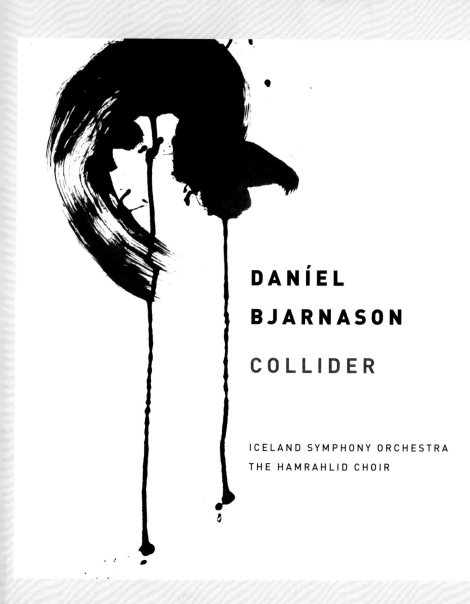

DANÍEL BJARNASON

COLLIDER

ICELAND SYMPHONY ORCHESTRA
THE HAMRAHLID CHOIR

Chris Bigg, album cover
for Daníel Bjarnason's
Collider,
Bedroom Community,
2018

Bigg can also be a master
of minimal composition,
yet still he maintains a
chance element – the
painterly curlicue all the
more expressive and
effective because of the
simplicity of the rest of
the cover.

that's quite good.'[3] In a blast of Duchampian lateral thought he picked it up and posted it to Andersen whose photographs levitate it to the status of iconic art object.

Deal liked the idea of the brick: 'everyone in some point in their life knows what a brick is, she enjoyed that aspect and the fact that you need a few to make something,'[4] says Bigg. It was the introduction of colour that cemented the final composition and gave the artwork a dynamic direction and a messed-up, angry energy of contrasting hues. So his sleeves are an organic series of creative steps based on intuitive notions of what more is needed and an implicit trust of each of the collaborators in each other, with the accidental leading the way.

Last year Bigg published Analogue Process, spanning work from his sketchbooks from 1987 to 2019. It is a cornucopia of graphic verve, errant typography and chance calligraphy. Here he is unfettered, running free, experimenting to his heart's content. It is a stunning look into the graphic alchemist's alembic and the magic that takes place there.

For Bigg this magic of the graphic design of music-related products is intensely exciting, an all-engrossing activity involving all the senses and finely tuning them to each new commission. It is particularly the record cover, its size, its tactility, its smell and its overriding symbiotic nature with the music inside it that is so swooningly evocative – a lifelong infatuation, but also a deep love.

Producing work of the intensity of Bigg's cannot be done with a cynical, mammon-obsessed heart, but only by playful, healthy respect for his art. It is from this emotional integrity that his work has evoked such impact – that and an eye for the detail. ◠

Notes
1. John Berger and Selçuk Demirel, *What Time Is It?*, Notting Hill Editions (London), 2019, p 99.
2. All quotes are from email correspondence between Chris Bigg and Neil Spiller in December 2019 unless otherwise stated.
3. Lucy Bourton, 'Chris Bigg Talks Us Through His Graphic Design for the Breeders' New Record', *It's Nice That*, 5 March 2018: www.itsnicethat.com/articles/chris-bigg-the-breeders-all-nerve-graphic-design-050318.
4. *Ibid*.

Kutan Ayata is a founding partner of Young & Ayata in New York City. He is a senior lecturer at the University of Pennsylvania in Philadelphia, and an adjunct assistant professor at the Pratt Institute Graduate Architecture and Urban Design (GAUD) programme in New York, teaching at graduate level. He received his Bachelor of Fine Arts in Architecture from the Massachusetts College of Art in Boston. He was a fellow at Princeton University School of Architecture in New Jersey, and earned his Master of Architecture degree in 2004 as a recipient of the Thesis Prize.

Ben van Berkel studied architecture at the Rietveld Academy in Amsterdam and at the Architectural Association (AA) in London, receiving the AA Diploma with Honours in 1987. In 1988 he and Caroline Bos set up UNStudio, an architectural practice in Amsterdam. UNStudio presents itself as a network of specialists in architecture, urban development and infrastructure. In 2018 he founded UNSense, an ArchTech company that designs and integrates human-centric tech solutions for the built environment. From 2011 to 2018 he held the Kenzo Tange Visiting Professor's Chair at the Harvard University Graduate School of Design (GSD) in Cambridge, Massachusetts.

Hernán Díaz Alonso is an Argentine-American architect, designer and educator. He is Director/Chief Executive Officer of the Southern California Institute of Architecture (SCI-Arc) in Los Angeles, and widely credited for spearheading its transition to digital technologies, playing a key role in shaping the school's graduate curriculum over the past decade. He is also the founder and principal of LA-based design practice HDA-X (formerly Xefirotarch), known for producing grotesque and sometimes unsettling work that challenges responses to the environment.

David Goldblatt is the author of *Art and Ventriloquism* (Routledge, 2005) and co-author of *Jazz and the Philosophy of Art* (Routledge, 2017). He is co-editor of *Aesthetics: A Reader in Philosophy of the Arts,* now in its fourth edition, and *The Aesthetics of Architecture: Philosophical Investigations into the Art of Building* (Wiley-Blackwell, 2011). He has published extensively in the field of aesthetics and was a contributor to Δ *Elegance* (Jan/Feb 2007) guest-edited by Ali Rahim and Hina Jamelle. He is emeritus professor of philosophy at Denison University in Granville, Ohio.

Thomas Heatherwick is a British designer whose prolific and varied work over two decades is characterised by its ingenuity, resulting in some of the most acclaimed designs of our time. Defying the conventional classification of design disciplines, he founded Heatherwick Studio in 1994 to bring the practices of design, architecture and urban planning together in a single workspace. The studio is currently working on approximately 30 projects in 10 countries, including 1000 Trees, a mixed-use development in Shanghai, and Google headquarters in California and London (in collaboration with BIG). Recently completed projects include the public centrepiece for New York's Hudson Yards, Zeitz Museum of Contemporary Art Africa in Cape Town, and the Coal Drops Yard retail district in London.

Ferda Kolatan is the co-founder and director of SU11 Architecture + Design, an award-winning practice in Brooklyn, New York, and an Associate Professor of Practice at the University of Pennsylvania Weitzman School of Design. SU11's projects have been published widely and exhibited at the Museum of Modern Art (MoMA) and PS1 in New York, Walker Art Center in Minneapolis, Vitra Design Museum in Weil am Rhein, Germany, Frac Centre in Orléans, France, and the Venice, Beijing and Istanbul biennales. He has published numerous articles on architecture and is co-author of the book *Meander: Variegating Architecture* (Bentley Institute Press, 2010).

Keke Li is a doctoral candidate at Tongji University in Shanghai where she collaborates with Professor Philip F Yuan to conduct research on the theory of computational design and digital fabrication, and the application of toolkits. Her work focuses on the intersection between computational design and generative programs, and she has published extensively on the study of generative design based on environmental performance.

Ascan Mergenthaler is a Senior Partner at Herzog & de Meuron. He studied architecture at Stuttgart University and the Bartlett School of Architecture, University College London (UCL). He has led the realisation of several international projects, including the de Young Museum in San Francisco, Parrish Art Museum on Long Island, Tate Modern Project in London, Elbphilharmonie in Hamburg, 56 Leonard Street in New York City, and the Tai Kwun centre for heritage and arts in Hong Kong. Among other projects, he is currently working on M+, a cultural centre for 20th- and 21st-century art in Hong Kong.

Philip Nobel is the Editorial Director of SHoP Architects and the author of *Sixteen Acres: Architecture and the Outrageous Struggle for the Future of Ground Zero* (Metropolitan Books, 2005). His writing has appeared in *Artforum*, the *New York Times*, *Metropolis*, the *London Review of Books* and elsewhere.

Antoine Picon is Professor of the History of Architecture and Technology at the Harvard University GSD. Trained as an engineer, architect and historian, he works on the history of architectural and urban technologies from the 18th century to the present, and has published extensively on this subject. He is the author of numerous publications, including *French Architects and Engineers in the Age of Enlightenment* (Cambridge University Press, 1992), *Digital Culture in Architecture* (Birkhäuser, 2010), and the Δ Primers *Ornament: The Politics of Architecture and Subjectivity* (2014) and *Smart Cities: A Spatialised Intelligence* (2015).

Paolo Pininfarina is the Chairman of Pininfarina, overseeing the international design company's commitment to design excellence. He joined Pininfarina in 1982, and in 1987 was appointed Chairman of Pininfarina Extra Srl, a Pininfarina Group company operating in the industrial, furnishing, architectural, nautical and aeronautical design sectors. Under his management, Pininfarina Extra has developed over 500 projects while consolidating relationships with prestigious international companies including Alenia Aermacchi, Bovet, Chivas Regal, Coca-Cola, Juventus, Lavazza, Motorola, Petronas, Samsung, Snaidero and Unilever.

M Casey Rehm is a multidisciplinary designer and founding partner of Los-Angeles-based Ishida Rehm Studio. He teaches at SCI-Arc, where he is the coordinator for the Master's of Science in Architectural Technology post-professional programme. He received his BArch from Carnegie Mellon University in Pittsburgh, Pennsylvannia, in 2005, and his Master of Science in Advanced Architecture from Columbia University in New York in 2009. He has professional experience practising in offices in LA, New York, Berlin and London on a range of works from low-income residential to large cultural projects.

Patrik Schumacher is principal of Zaha Hadid Architects (ZHA) and has led the firm since Zaha Hadid's passing in 2016. He joined her in 1988 and was seminal in developing ZHA to become a global brand. He studied philosophy, mathematics and architecture in Bonn, Stuttgart and London, and received his PhD at the Institute for Cultural Science in Klagenfurt, Austria. In 1996 he founded the Design Research Laboratory at the AA in London where he continues to teach. He also taught design studios at the University of Applied Arts Vienna with Zaha Hadid from 2000 to 2015, and is currently teaching a PhD group there.

Neil Spiller is Editor of Ⅾ, and was previously Hawksmoor Chair of Architecture and Landscape and Deputy Pro Vice Chancellor at the University of Greenwich, London. Prior to this he was Vice Dean at the Bartlett School of Architecture, UCL. He has made an international reputation as an architect, designer, artist, teacher, writer and polemicist. He is the founding director of the Advanced Virtual and Technological Architecture Research (AVATAR) group, which continues to push the boundaries of architectural design and discourse in the face of the impact of 21st-century technologies. Its current preoccupations include augmented and mixed realities and other metamorphic technologies.

Paolo Trevisan is the Head of Design and Architecture of Pininfarina of America, where he spearheads the firm's expansion into the fields of architecture and interior design. Joining Pininfarina in Italy in 2000, he worked as the Chief Design Manager overseeing a range of projects from graphics and packaging to architecture, interiors and transportation, including nautical, aeronautical and people movers. He also served as Master Coordinator at the Istituto Europeo di Design and as a jury member of the Associazione per il Disegno Industriale. Under his management, Pininfarina of America's architecture projects have won important international awards, including the 2019 International Architecture Award for its Cyrela residential tower in São Paulo.

Philip F Yuan is the founder of Shanghai-based Archi-Union Architects and Fab-Union Technology, and a professor at Tongji University. His research and practice involve the application of prototypical methods and advanced manufacturing techniques, and focus on how digital tools offer the possibility of a new authorship for today's architects based on an understanding of culture, materials and the built environment. His projects have received many international awards, have been exhibited worldwide, including at the Venice Architectural Biennale, Chicago Biennial, Milan Triennial, Shenzhen / Hong Kong Bi-City Biennale and the Shanghai Biennale, and have formed parts of several renowned museum collections.

What is Architectural Design?

Founded in 1930, *Architectural Design* (Δ) is an influential and prestigious publication. It combines the currency and topicality of a newsstand journal with the rigour and production qualities of a book. With an almost unrivalled reputation worldwide, it is consistently at the forefront of cultural thought and design.

Issues of Δ are edited either by the journal's Editor, Neil Spiller, or by an invited Guest-Editor. Renowned for being at the leading edge of design and new technologies, Δ also covers themes as diverse as architectural history, the environment, interior design, landscape architecture and urban design.

Provocative and pioneering, Δ inspires theoretical, creative and technological advances. It questions the outcome of technical innovations as well as the far-reaching social, cultural and environmental challenges that present themselves today.

For further information on Δ, subscriptions and purchasing single issues see:

https://onlinelibrary.wiley.com/journal/15542769

Volume 89 No 5
ISBN 978 1119 546245

Volume 89 No 6
ISBN 978 1119 546214

Volume 90 No 1
ISBN 978 1119 540038

Volume 90 No 2
ISBN 978 1119 555094

Volume 90 No 3
ISBN 978 1119 617563

Volume 90 No 4
ISBN 978 1119 576440